~   READING the VOICE

READING the VOICE

~ *Native American Oral Poetry on the Page*

Paul G. Zolbrod

UNIVERSITY OF UTAH PRESS
Salt Lake City

Library of Congress Cataloging-in-Publication Data

Zolbrod, Paul G.
    Reading the voice : native American oral poetry on the
page / Paul G. Zolbrod.
        p.   cm.
    Includes bibliographical references.
    ISBN 0–87480–457–4 (alk. paper)
    1. Indian poetry—North America—History and criticism.
2. Oral tradition—North America—History and criticism.
I. Title.
PM168.Z65   1995
398.2′08997—dc20   94–42708

CONTENTS

Preface   vii

1   Introduction   1
A Working Hypothesis
Poetry and Related Terms
Poetry and the Sacred

2   Sacred Texts and Iroquois Culture: A Case Study   22
The Story of Creation
The Thank-You Prayer
The Dekanawida Myth
The Condolence Ritual
Poetry as a Cultural Institution

3   Classifying Poetic Texts: Voice   34
Two Kinds of Voice
The Lyric Voice in Print
The Colloquial Voice and the Printed Page

4   Classifying Poetic Texts: Mode   81
The Dramatic Mode
The Narrative Mode

5   Toward a Taxonomy of Texts   108

Glossary of Key Terms   125
Notes   133
Bibliography   139

PREFACE

THIS IS A BOOK about poetry: about its sacred underpinnings, its broad presence in everyday life, its necessity to the human community—all of which go largely unnoticed as the printed word and literature move insidiously away from wide public view. More topically, this book is about poetry's abiding importance among Native Americans from ancient times to the present—going back long before Europe's alphabetical technology transformed much of this continent's poetry and song from the unamplified, unrecorded product of the speaking or singing voice into something inscribed silently on paper. This volume seeks connections between an ancient tribal way of making and diffusing poetry and more up-to-date, print-oriented or electronic ways.

I make no pretense at completing the task I begin here. Instead I consider this work a tentative first step in reconciling mainstream America with the deep poetic roots of an unwritten aboriginal past, perhaps even with the deeper European roots of its own ancient poetic traditions. Maybe the time has come to try placing Native American poetry in such a perspective. I merely wish to propose one possible way of doing so.

As attention to the "literature" of Native Americans mounts, that term requires reexamination, as does its sister term "poetry." Otherwise we stand to miss much that is essential to the verbal art of the people once carelessly called "Indians," and to that of other indigenous peoples whom print cultures approach from an alien perspective. Also overlooked might be an alternative way of appreciating our own poetry and the long traditions it too essentially bears, especially as electronic media begin to supplant ordinary print. Or, to put the matter more simply, by redefining the term "poetry," by considering the way Native Americans first produced it, and by examining techniques for reproducing it, we might recover a broadly maintained poetic awareness otherwise subdued by the merger of print with digital technology or restricted to an exclusionary academic setting.

I COULD NEITHER have conceived of this book nor written it without help of all kinds. I must first acknowledge the generous support I received during my thirty years on the faculty of Allegheny College, spanning four presidents and nearly eight generations of undergraduates. In the early 1970s—long before multiculturalism became a central issue on college campuses—I experimented with a course in ethnopoetics there, encouraged by the faculty and the administration along with class after class of curious, open-minded students. For nearly twenty years thereafter, they and colleagues alike helped me to remain skeptical of standard ways of reading literature and modestly aware of how little we actually know about the alphabet as a means of recording the human voice.

Not enough recognition goes to how a small college setting can stimulate innovative investigation. For one thing, specialization does not isolate researchers from each other or a wider community. For another, there is a freedom to raise naive questions among colleagues without fear of being considered ill-informed. In that spirit I wish to mention I. Lloyd Michaels and James Bulman from my own department of English, along with Bruce Clayton from history—all for their abiding friendship and willingness to listen and to share their own unique ideas as I tried to fashion a cohesive way to deal with material new to me and sometimes strange to them. I also cite Glen Rodgers, professor of Chemistry at Allegheny, who helped me gain a perspective I might otherwise not have acquired. I express as well my gratitide to the trustees and administration at Allegheny for providing money and time to allow field research and writing. And I would be remiss if I were to overlook the wider community of Meadville, Pennsylvania, where Allegheny is located. Whether at the public library or the local historical society, with various civic groups and service clubs, or among area farmers and teachers willing to talk about books they read or poems they wrote, I was able to find ordinary citizens eager to talk and listen as I explored material unrecognized by literary academicians at the time.

Given my growing interest in the oral traditions of Native Americans, I learned that the study of poetry can occur out of books and away from the classroom. In considering that, I pause to recognize the people who gathered at the Cold Spring Longhouse on the Allegany Seneca Reservation in upstate New York, and to recall in particular the warmth and hospitality I experienced during my frequent visits to the home of Avery and Fidelia Jimerson during an early phase of my study. The two of them have long since "passed on," as Navajos say about the deceased, but their spirit truly lives on. I have vivid memories of Fidelia dancing as Avery drummed and sang long into the evening in their modest kitchen, and of his laughter as she served me a heaping portion of parboiled milkweed pod and urged that I at least try it. From my friendship with them I learned things about poetry and song that graduate school had never revealed.

Turning to the Navajos, among whom I have lived and worked and studied for many years now, I could never hope to name all whose help has enriched my life personally and professionally. Literally hundreds of them have welcomed me in chapter houses, hogans, private homes, classrooms, tribal offices, trading posts, pastures, and corrals. With a uniform generosity they have shared stories and songs with me, answered questions often before I got around to asking them, and softened my clumsy intrusions with uncanny patience and tact. I wish I had the space to mention them all, but I must single out a few whose help and friendship have been especially significant—with profound apologies to those I should likewise mention but simply cannot. They include my erstwhile teacher, long-standing friend, and able collaborator Roseann Willink, originally from Pueblo Pintado, New Mexico, and currently on the linguistics faculty at the University of New Mexico. She has been pivotal to whatever success I can claim as an interpreter of Navajo poetry and culture. I offer special thanks as well to Blackhorse Mitchell—author, educator, and Windway singer from Shiprock, New Mexico, for his lucid guidance through the intricacies of Navajo ceremonialism. And I pay special tribute to Loretta Binally of Crown Point, New Mexico, along with her children, her grandchildren, her great-grandchildren, and everyone else in her extended family who has participated in making me one of them. Among them, too, I have discovered poetic depths not easily plumbed in a conventional academic setting.

Assembling this volume actually got underway during the summer of 1991 at the D'Arcy McNickle Center for Native American History, Newberry Library, Chicago, where I presided over a workshop on sacred Native American texts with twenty college teachers from all over the country. Among other things, I wanted to get them to align religion and workaday life with poetry and then question whether it perforce had to be written down to exist. By responding with an open mind they helped me secure the paradigm I propose here. I thank them for the opportunity of testing my sometimes unconventional and unorthodox ideas about poetry.

Prior to that gathering, I spent a sabbatical year at the Laboratory of Anthropology, Museum of Indian Arts and Culture, in Santa Fe. For some time I had been thinking about the distinctions I try to forge here, although I never attempted to put them on paper until I began preparing for the Chicago workshop while in residence at the Museum. For valuable help while there, I thank the entire staff, especially Steve Becker and Bruce Bernstein, Director and Associate Director, respectively, along with Museum Librarian Laura Holt, whose professional skill I found unmatched among all the libraries and archives where I have done research. I cite as well Steve Lekson, who then served as State Archaeologist; Edmund Ladd, Curator of Ethnology; and Curtis Schaafsma, Curator of Anthropology, for the way they listened and made comments on what I was doing. Special appreciation goes as well to Katherine Spencer Halpern and John Adair, senior scholars whose guidance and encouragement have been considerable. Together with them I single out Dr. Joanne McCloskey for helping me with field techniques, for adding to my understanding of Navajo life and culture, for listening patiently and carefully, and for the very special bond that has grown between us.

Following my term at the Museum, the workshop resulted in a small monograph published by the Newberry Library under the title, *Sacred Texts, Occasional Papers in the Curriculum No. 14.*

Fred Hoxie, then Director of the D'Arcy McNickle Center, read a preliminary draft of that early work and helped me prepare it for publication with the assistance of Harvey Markowitz, Assistant Director at the time, in a process that allowed me to crystalize my thinking even more. My thanks go as well to Jeff Grathwohl, senior editor at the University of Utah Press, who read a preliminary draft of an expanded version of what I submitted to the Newberry Library, and thereafter guided me through added revisions. A. L. Soens, Professor of English at the University of Notre Dame, and Professor Julian Rice of Florida Atlantic University, read the resulting draft and offered helpful suggestions. To them I am also grateful.

My final word of acknowledgement comes as something of an indulgence. At my suggestion, Mr. Grathwohl consented to send a copy of a late draft of this work to my daughter, Zoe Zolbrod, who was then getting her start as an editor. Her comments were crisp, unsparing, trenchant and hence enormously helpful. I monitored them carefully, alternately humbled by her skill and made proud by how professionally she handled her father's work. For all of its shortcomings, this is a better book as a result, and I dedicate it to her both with a parent's love and an author's gratitude for such sterling editorial assistance.

None of the people or institutions mentioned above bear any responsibility for whatever errors and shortcomings may persist. To the contrary, without their help and guidance this would have been a lesser enterprise by far.

ONE

Introduction

A Working Hypothesis

THIS VOLUME OFFERS an introductory framework for examining what has been called America's "first literature" (Hymes: 1987, p. 80). Technically, Native American oral poetry may well be called literature, since much of it has found its way into print. Much of it has not yet been written, however, so I prefer to find a more accurate term for naming the oral traditions still in use to perpetuate the living poetry of Native Americans. For even when such material is reproduced on the page by today's growing list of scholar-translators, it remains fundamentally a creation of the speaking or singing voice heard by listeners as a social transaction. It is not necessarily composed alphabetically and indelibly printed in the way that Europe's literature is. Instead it develops by way of a more elastic oral transmission, which means that it is made to be heard again and again over a lifetime. Furthermore, it can vary widely with each retelling whereas a literary work acquires its authenticity in fixed, unchanging permanence.

Hence traditional Native American material is not literature strictly speaking, at least not in its origins. Even if it is packaged by translators as something to read, those who come to it by way of books must do so conscious of the sounds of speech and song, by reading the voice, as it were, instead of an inert, silent sheet of paper full of alphabetical symbols.

In starting with that suggestion I bring no fixed theoretical position to this project save for offering a few opening definitions followed by a simple if somewhat speculative taxonomy. I do not seek to sidestep the intricate dialectics of postmodern thought. Rather, I hope to subsume them into a clearer kind of synthesis that can allow any reader or listener or viewer to identify a poetic experience and describe its effects to any desired degree of simplicity or complexity. Nor do I seek to advance any particular approach borrowed from Anglo-European sources, whether as early as Plato and Aristotle or as recent as Foucault and Derrida or Bakhtin and Lyotard. Insofar as it is possible for an outsider to do so, I wish to examine traditional Native American material from within, according to its own manner of composition, its medium of transmission, and its original purpose. Maybe then it can be compared with mainstream literature and possibly even used to deepen the appreciation of Europe's print-driven legacy. First, though, we need to build a tentative framework for understanding an ongoing Native American poetic legacy more deeply than current popular conceptions allow.

My working hypothesis is that the verbalized world view of a culture has roots in a shared sacred vision of the universe. That view then helps to shape the community's social organization in the broadest terms—incorporating its history, its polity, its educational system, and its artistic and ceremonial life—while at the same time affecting individual participants in it. Ultimately that speculation on my part becomes a literary statement, at least by the conventional and implicitly print-bourne European standards of what makes for literature. For I place a certain primacy on the poetry of any people and in doing so assert the centrality to it of their traditional sacred texts. Even at a time when the Western world's great literary texts are being challenged for articulating a credo of imperial dominion, they nonetheless combine to define European tradition down to its biblical and Hellenic origins, which are rooted in accounts of the world's inception, human origin, and divine intervention in the lives of mortals.

Every culture possesses a bigger-than-life creation story like the Hawaiian *Kumulipo* or the Mayan *Popol Vuh* and has fashioned a poetic way of telling it. The Western world's Old Testament Genesis and Hesiod's retelling of *The Theogeny* are two obvious familiar examples, which have in turn inspired subsequent poets—like Dante, Shakespeare, and Milton, or Emily Dickinson, James Joyce, and Paul Claudel, who are drawn centripetally to the Western world's primary myths and religious themes. Furthermore, a culture also sustains an attendant body of ceremonial discourse including prayers, chants, stories, and the like. Allowing for certain religious underpinnings to today's international consumer culture, we may even agree to include the language of such items as popular song lyrics or tv commercials as examples or partial illustrations. Creation narratives and the complex of poetic works they engender are fundamental to what emerges as a poetic tradition of a people, which predicates what lies at the heart of all that emerges palpably as their culture.

To build my framework, I must first attempt to redefine a few old terms whose familiar use has weakened them, especially for their usefulness in introducing work whose origins differ as much as Native American poetic discourse apparently does from mainstream European literature. In putting those terms in a new perspective, and in constructing a rudimentary classification to recognize sacred Native American texts, I draw from over twenty years of archival research and reservation fieldwork in search of tribal activity that projects ongoing preliterate traditions. I also draw from over thirty years of introducing undergraduates to what we continue to call literature: on the one hand they become progressively less inclined to read it, especially outside the college classroom; and on the other, we have begun recognizing orally transmitted alternatives to it, whether from recorded song lyrics or a revived interest in preliterate sources. I also relent to a few basic structuralist principles—which I will apply in a later chapter—to secure distinctions that it seems ought to be attempted as electronic media compete more and more with print for the attention of students and the public alike.

To nonacademic readers the reference to structuralism may seem too remote; to today's academic scholars and critics it may sound objectionable, if not outdated. According to the redoubtable M. H. Abrams, whose definitions of literary terms provide something of a standard, structuralism views "all social and cultural phenomena," including literary texts, "as a signifying structure." It "undertakes to explain how the phenomena have achieved their significance... by reference to an underlying system" that can be seen and described objectively as a fixed set "of rules and codes" (Abrams, pp. 280–81). "Much structuralist analysis is *formalist* in the sense of separating *form* and *content* and giving form priority," adds Raymond Williams (p. 306). Seen as a movement, structuralism gave way to a "poststructuralist" attack on "the quasi-scientific pretensions" of its "strict form" (Abrams, p. 258). During the closing decades of the twentieth century academic critics and theorists have tended largely to deny the earlier structuralists' "claims for the existence of self-evident foundations that guarantee the validity of knowledge and truth," Abrams continues. "This antifoundationalism, conjoined with skepticism about traditional conceptions of meaning and knowledge, is evident in some exponents of almost all modes of current literary studies" (pp. 258–59).

I consider structuralism an approach that originally claimed to make neutral contrasts possible, which is what I seek in these polemical times. I recognize that structuralist objectivity can imply a rigidity that permits no alternative points of view, and that it is said to feed "complicity with imperialism" and help to maintain "the doctrine of objectivism, and the credo of monumentalism" (Rosaldo, p. 34). At its worst structuralism may indeed have abetted all that, but at its best it can still highlight useful contrasts with systematic neutrality; and for my part, I cling to the conviction that objectivity is an ideal that must always be sought and need not be made an instrument for power or oppression.

Please bear in mind, then, that as I attempt to hammer out some basic distinctions, I want to avoid making value judgments. I wish to speak speculatively rather than assertively: the material dealt with here is relatively unfamiliar and awaits an accurate, serviceable paradigm. Among other things, its discovery offers new ways of examining poetry, of synthesizing poetic and religious expression, and of recognizing the centrality of something sacred even in cultures like our own, which appear to have grown increasingly irreligious. Given that newness, what I offer is a tentative start at best. For now, I can only touch on points that require more amplification than I am able to give because of limitations of space or constraints on what I myself know. I welcome any amplification or disagreement that will lead to a fuller, more accurate way of dealing with texts grounded in sacred vision that come out of Native American cultures, whether as religion, as poetic expression, as history and protohistory, or as pure ethnographic data.

Poetry and Related Terms

As a start I would like to develop a working understanding of three main terms and two sets of subterms, as it were. The first of the three broadly generic terms I wish to define is *literature*. Traditionally, it has been employed rather loosely to include a number of similarly broad genres of written discourse including what is conventionally identified as poetry, fiction, and drama—each of which could be subdivided in a variety of ways. Thus we might have free, blank, or lyric verse; or we might distinguish between the short story and the novel, sometimes placing the novella or short novel between them in distinguishing narrative fiction from factual stories; and to the repertoire of plays, whether published or produced, today we might add films or at least screenplays and even video scripts, although such items have yet to make their way fully into the pantheon of written texts that have gained at least tacit recognition for possessing certain aesthetic or conceptual properties.

More by assumption than by deliberate designation, then, the term *literature*, as we tend to use it, exists by and large in association with print. The etymology of the term, in fact, summons images of parchment or paper, of alphabetical systems whether hand wrought or letterpress, and of electronically applied print technology. *The Oxford Dictionary of English Etymology* traces the term *literature* through French to the Latin *literatura*, meaning "alphabetic letters, linguistic science, grammar, and learning." In a more elaborate discussion of what the word *literature* means in the framework of Western civilization, Raymond Williams, in *Keywords* (pp. 183–88), associates literature primarily with alphabetical and print technologies. Gradually, it "was specialized towards imaginative writing," displacing the term *poetry*, which in the Renaissance served that distinctive function. More recently, he suggests, the word *literature* may have generalized enough to include newer modes of transmission through broadcasting and electronic media. In his effort to distinguish between written and oral traditions, William Bright suggests that the term "refers roughly to that body of discourses or texts which, within any society, is considered worthy of dissemination, transmission, and preservation in essentially constant form" (p. 80).

It turns out, however, that the term *literature* has limitations precisely because it presupposes existence on the printed page (or more recently on reels and tape) and hence precludes thoughtful reference to any orally-transmitted verbal artifact—if I may use that term—containing manifest poetic qualities. Our customary use of the word *literature*, with its implicitly restricted reference to alphabetically transmitted material, has blinded us to the possibility that poetry might exist beyond the margins of the printed page, and perhaps even to features that print has managed to subdue by its silence. After all, books do not themselves speak; they merely utilize an elaborate network of symbols as a graphic representation of the human voice. Overlooking that basic relationship all but eliminates recognition that people like the Navajos in the American Southwest or the Maori of New Zealand might have produced anything genuinely poetic without the use of print. Casually restricting the term *poetry* to a subspecies of literature implies that items like the Anglo-Saxon *Beowulf*—to say nothing of the preliterate traditions that eventually fed into what we now call the Bible or Homeric material—added no poetic dimensions to the lives of people who recited them before any sort of alphabetical technology was available to record and preserve them.

To be sure, differences exist between written poetic discourse and oral, as Paul Zumthor points out in *Oral Poetry: An Introduction*—a work that deserves wider notice among literary critics than it has apparently so far received. He recognizes above all the permanence of print that makes written poetry appear fixed, while unwritten performances allow for an elasticity whose apparent impermanence makes oral poetry seem less refined for those who limit their poetic experience to reading (p. 99). Likewise, "a long written work may be drafted in fits and starts whereas the oral one has no rough drafts." Moreover, "the listener" to an oral performance "follows the thread; no going back is possible." Distinctions are many and carry with them some fascinating implications; they call for a fuller discussion than I can offer here and a far more systematic exploration than Zumthor makes, although he still provides an admirably detailed examination. Nevertheless, the two categories, respectively, of written and unwritten verbal activity clearly remain allied species of the genus *poetry*, parallel in their attainment of "a specific eloquence" and "an ease in diction and phrasing," along with "a power of suggestion: an overarching of predominance of rhythms," among other traits that compel readers and listeners alike to pay attention in whatever ways these two techniques of delivery require (Zumthor, p. 98). The language of poetry abides as much in a live performance as it does on the inert page.

For that reason, I would like to revert somewhat to the old Renaissance notion and replace the term *literature* with the older, more serviceable term *poetry*, which I would broadly designate as the genus and call *literature* one species of it. Making it the second more broadly generic term in my list of definitions, then, I'd define poetry as that art form whose primary medium is language, whether written or spoken (or sung); whether recorded in print, on video or audio tape, or whether packaged in the human memory according to various mnemonic techniques (see Finnegan, Goody, Havelock, [1963, 1978] Lord; see also Mallery and Gelb). In that regard, poetry may coexist with material devices, such as petroglyphs or petrographs common the world over, with Germanic runes or with Iroquois wampum, among other material things used to assist the individual or collective memory.

Poetry, then, becomes an art form as readily oral as written. Oral poetry can be distinguished as fundamentally transmitted by way of the human voice and monitored by the ear. Only secondarily is it recorded and distributed through the medium of print and, more recently, through electronic media. Written (or alphabetical) poetry may then be differentiated according to whether it is originally composed in manuscript form and whose spoken dimension occurs as it were secondarily (see Levenston, p. 10), or whether it was harvested from an oral performance, put into print, and in that written form outlived or outdistanced whoever recited it for an audience of listeners. A finer distinction that designates poetry once oral and now retained only through writing need not be of concern just yet, however; Levenston undertakes a viable exploration of it in *The Stuff of Literature*, and I will return to it later.

What makes speech artistic and hence identifiable as poetry remains an unanswered question, if not unanswerable.[1] Likewise, it is difficult to specify what makes any medium of expression artistic. I will return later to that point, too; but for now, let me say simply and initially that art can occur with the imposition of patterns whatever the medium, so that seeking linguistic design is central to the issue of attributing poetry to voice as readily as to print, just as design reveals some deeper, more purely conceptual quality in any art. When I speak of design, in fact, I have in mind some inner conception of order that somehow finds orderly expression on the surface of the work, no matter what the medium.

Focusing on poetry as the verbal art in his effort to distinguish between written and oral "literature," William Bright proposes this definition: "a poem is a text in which linguistic form—phonological, syntactic, and lexical—is organized in such a way as to carry aesthetic content which is at least as important, as regards the response of the receiver, as is the cognitive content carried by the same text" (p. 82). To that, let me also add something that Zumthor points out in his effort to distinguish "oral *poetry*" from "the more extensive notion *oral literature*" that "is beginning to infiltrate the ranks of the scholarly" (p. 32; the italics are his). Oral poetry, he specifies, "is distinguished by the intensity of its features; it is rigorously formalized, replete with markings of a very evident structuration" (p. 33). There again, then, we find recognition of design, or of order—call it what you will.

All of which prompts the examination of two sets of distinct subterms mentioned earlier. Defining them might more easily permit the recognition of poetic material that Native Americans have produced. The first set includes *electronic poetry*—such as a film, for example, or an audio or video recording—and the *printed poetry* conventionally positioned in books and periodicals, to-gether with *recited poetry*—as at a Navajo Kinaaldá ceremony, for example, or at a family commencement gathering in a Nav-ajo community, or else at something like the San Juan Rain God Drama.

I cite these two examples in particular because I was able to per-ceive firsthand how recited poetry functions in two distinct con-texts at ceremonial gatherings. In late March 1991, I attended my first Kinaaldá or traditional girl's puberty ceremony at Bicenti—seven miles north of Crown Point, New Mexico. A traditional medicine man presided over the night-long culmination of a four-day event marking the occasion of the first menses of two first cousins—in effect, their entry into womanhood. Consisting of a series of standard chants and prayers from the Blessingway cycle that arises from the Navajo creation story (see Wyman: 1970, es-pecially pp. 407–59), his words are recited where and whenever he performs in fixed patterns of meter and style characteristic of ritual drama throughout the Southwest (see Frisbie).

Later that spring, I was invited to a family gathering to mark the graduation of yet another cousin from high school. During the course of the evening, every relative stood and offered a speech marking the event. As an invited family friend and hence some-thing of a family member myself in the Navajo way of reckoning affinal relationships, even I was obliged to contribute. Conscious of the happy solemnity of the occasion, I expressed myself with a guarded care that hopefully measured up to the eloquence of what others were saying. The round of orations opened and closed with a recitation by the graduate's maternal grandmother and paternal grandfather, respectively. Both spoke in Navajo, as did the young man's parents and his elder relatives.

While they spoke extemporaneously—unlike the medicine man at the Kinaaldá, whose songs and prayers were not his own but lyrics long established as the ceremony's central discourse—they referred frequently to the Blessingway and couched their own words in the established cadences manifest in the Kinaaldá, sometimes adopting entire phrases from some of its lyrics, and lyrics similar to it, to fill out a line rhythmically. In effect, then, the whole round of speeches was framed by the formal recitation of these two most venerable guests. I hasten to add as well that their speeches in particular were moving and powerful, bringing tears to the eyes of many of the others. As he himself gave his oration—which he delivered in English—the graduate too had obviously absorbed and mastered this ceremonial rhetoric and adapted it to another language. Listening to him and the others— especially the two grandparents—I recognized once again what I had already learned to perceive at Navajo gatherings: these are people whose poetry resides more in what they recite than in anything they might write down; and for them, poetry can be an applied art. Print is still too new among them to reflect their traditional reliance on recited poetic discourse.

Such examples of poetic recitation at work in an oral setting stand apart from poetry transmitted electronically and stored on reels, discs, and tapes and film, for example, or from that which circulates on the bound page or might be pulled out of a data base on a computer.[2] Electronic poetry more often than not gives the illusion of being recited spontaneously, although it usually comes from a written script and hence qualifies as literature in the strict, letter-oriented sense of the term. Printed poetry, it seems to me, like the broader category of literature, is marked by a certain intentionality that can be applied more deliberately than an oral poetry might apply it. In an oral setting the performer is more likely to subordinate him or herself to the tradition represented by the work; the writer, able to work more slowly and ponderously, can more readily manipulate language as it gradually materializes on the page. In their discussion of how scriptures became literature, Gabel and Wheeler explore that process (see especially pp. 3–15). The Bible, they explain, consists of a varied body of material consciously transmitted to the written page long after the facts. To cite one example, they consider why the "so-called Priestly authors, who were supposedly responsible" for producing a written version of creation, apparently chose to prefix "their account to an already existing account of Adam and Eve in the Garden of Eden." Evidently "they themselves appreciated the validity of differing points of view" and saw value in offering those who were to read the story "more than one perspective . . ." (pp. 6–7). And they go on to explain how, in their estimation, the redaction that becomes

Scriptures represents a process of deliberate reflection quite unlike the more spontaneous discourse of oral performance.

The second set of terms I wish to treat permits another useful
distinction. What is conventionally called poetry might better be
called *verse*—at least when we refer to printed poetry. Because
the formal patterns of verse are generally more rigidly structured
(the iambic pentameter blank verse of Milton or Wordsworth, for
example; the rhyming heroic couplets of Dryden or Pope; or the
paced alterations of length in the lines and the stanzas of an ode
by Shelley or Keats), when stored in print it is carefully arrayed
on the page with wide, ragged right-hand margins. Contrast that
with *prose*, which more closely resembles vernacular speech in being less rigidly patterned and which is therefore packaged on the
page margin to margin and in a way that does not call attention to
patterns of meter and rhyme or subpatterns of measured sound
and/or syntax in the way that traditional verse does. Or as Levenston more succinctly puts it, "If it is printed in lines, it is poetry; if
in paragraphs, it is prose" (p. 2).

Which brings me to a third subset of terms, beginning with
text. During what might be called the golden age of print, which
began in the early nineteenth century as literacy spread in North
America and England (see Altick, for example)—and which is
probably pretty well over in this heavily electronic age—that
term referred to printed poetry or what has conventionally been
called *literature*. Now we need to widen it, too. Zumthor calls a
text "an organized linguistic sequence"; and very likely the process of organizing the sequence presupposes some kind of awareness that the sequence ought to be preserved graphically (p. 41;
see also p. 61). If we can apply *text* that broadly, perhaps we can
use it to designate the way in which poetry is stored, whether as
originally printed, as Shakespeare's plays were or the way Chaucer hand-produced his *Canterbury Tales*; whether harvested from
a preliterate tradition in the manner of *The Odyssey* or *The Iliad*,
or as *Beowulf* is likely to have been (see Lord, Magoun); or
whether assembled electronically as a recording, a video production, or a film.[3]

We could perhaps gain breadth and accuracy combined by using
the term that way and thus speak of a written text; of recorded

texts, whether audio or video; of a cinematext in the case of film. As a useful concept for expanding the purview of poetry, we could broaden it further the way Brotherston indicates Derrida does (Brotherston, p. 42; see also Derrida, p. 136) and possibly even speak of a ceremonial text, which implies storage by memory, custom, or ritual as in something like the Navajo *Nightway Chant* (see Faris); or as with a Protestant wedding ceremony, a Jewish bar mitzvah, or a Roman Catholic Mass, which combine elements of written text with components of memorized or formulaic verbal ritual. Here I am primarily concerned with printed texts and with how print may best be utilized in transforming written texts out of ceremonial material acquired from oral traditions throughout tribal North America, although I would also like to arouse speculation about the possibility of storing ceremonial texts electronically, as well as graphically via the printed page.

Poetry and the Sacred

MOVING AWAY FROM subsets, the third broadly generic term I'd like to explore is the word *sacred*. Explaining its meaning seems absolutely daunting, yet to appreciate the oral poetry of tribal peoples requires an understanding of the sacrosanct that reaches beyond the familiar confines of the Judeo-Christian complex of religions. To be fully understood, any body of poetry requires a recognition of its cultural setting; and because preliterate non-Western cultures do not necessarily distinguish between secular and religious, a broad grasp of the sacred independent of narrower biblical concerns helps to place the material to be discussed below in a cultural context free of any sectarian biases the Old Testament legacy so actively transmitted throughout the Western world, even among those who profess no Jewish, Christian, or Islamic formal ties.

I have as yet no firm definition of the *sacred* of my own to suggest: it is foolish enough to try to define the term *poetry*, and the *sacred* is, if anything, even more difficult to encapsulate. Yet some kind of agreed-upon understanding is needed, especially since the poetry that nonliterate, tribal peoples produce goes largely unrecognized in the literate community, as does the existence of anything genuinely sacramental lying outside the parameters of the world's major institutionalized faiths. More than that, there needs to be a renewed awareness of what poetry accomplishes in any culture, including those that have relied on print as early as so-called Old World cultures have. Having first limited their recognition of the poetic to written texts and then divorced the ideas of the sacred and the poetic, those European language communities no longer see poetry as central to their culture. Instead, it becomes seemingly incidental to institutionalized activities like commerce and production and the law.

Once we overcome the sectarian limitations of the Old Testament religions, it becomes easier to see how Native American oral poetry and that of other tribal peoples overlap with the sacred. Only then can we deal fully with the deep spiritual underpinnings of poetry shared in oral performance among people whose vision of earth and cosmos is neither narrowly Judeo-Christian nor fully secular in the general understanding of temporality. If Native American tribal poetry is to be placed in some kind of workably enlarged awareness of what poetry really is, its spiritual dimensions must be properly acknowledged. That should be a joint effort among many rather than a responsibility I would presume to undertake alone, which means widening established religious horizons. I merely wish to start by adding some observations of my own on what makes for the sacred to a few corollary observations that others have made. Perhaps other critics will follow suit by applying broadened religious conceptions of their own to poetry which only at first appears secular.

In presenting material to her for the San Juan Rain God Drama, wherein rain-bringing deities are summoned from the farthest reaches of the known world of the Tewa Pueblos, Vera Laski's informant Shaayet'aan (or Striped Stone Fetish) cautioned her that "the purpose of our ceremonies is not entertainment but attainment; namely the attainment of the *Good Life* [italics in the original]. Our dramas, our songs, and our dances are not performed for fun as they might be in the white man's world; no, they are more than that: they are the very essence of our lives; they are sacred" (Laski, p. 2). Elsewhere, Laski herself comments that "whether or not a dance is to be called a kachina ceremony depends on the inner attitude, the spiritual approach of the dancer, and the intensity of feeling rather than on the outward presence of masks and paints" (p. 24).

In other words, essentially human internal qualities such as spiritual intensity help to give external reality its sacred dimension. Clouds thus become manifestations of kachinas or spirit-beings in the desert Southwest. Likewise, for people like the Hopis or the Navajos living where moisture is scarce, lack of rain can be internalized by an entire group: each individual experiences the same arid conditions and feels the same anxiety more or less. All may wonder what they alone might have done to "deserve" such a threat, or what they as individuals might help others do to propitiate the forces that summon clouds and bring rain. The resulting intensity can then generate a communal expression for those who share it, materializing ritually as kachinas or other rain-bringing supernaturals sung or spoken of in public recitation.

To cite Clifford Geertz with a mixture of paraphrase and quotation, in constructing a shared sacred conception of the external, a society draws from the "sense of intrinsic obligation" that its individual members maintain, and from the "deep moral seriousness" of each. Its people build a world view out of their picture of "the way things in sheer actuality are, to create their concept of nature, of self, of society." Rain gods must be propitiated the way people themselves sometimes must be. Surveying and synthesizing what can be seen and known on a phenomenal level, members of a community unite in conceptualizing "their most comprehensive ideas of order" (pp. 421–22). Thereby the sacred world of unseen forces projected outside the self grows out of an intense devotion experienced within it, resulting in an established conception of order and organization—somewhat analogous, I might add, to the order and organization that a practicing poet, whether alphabetical or oral, must impose on language. Effigies and verbal artifacts alike become tangible expressions of something deeply felt.

In endorsing that link between internal and external, Karl Luckert recognizes that most such constructs are responses to "greater-than-human reality configurations," or "greater-than-human personages or gods" (1976, p. 5). It is humans however who remain the unit of comparing that greatness and who respond to it, so that "wherever 'personhood' is being recognized as the quality which raises man above the animal level . . . any so-conceived greater-than-human reality must possess at least the human quantity of personal qualities" (ibid.). Thus an apprehension of what is greater-than-human or other-than-human requires a firm grasp of what is human jointly conceived by individuals aware that they share with others a felt intensity within one's own being. There, too, the centrally located inner self connects with some outside force which is greater than ordinary nature discloses.

Even the greater-than-human, godlike supernaturals are given fundamentally human traits by the poets who invoke them or attempt to depict them—often buttressed by similes, metaphors, and other tropes that help secure the connection. According to traditional Seneca narratives, marauding stone giants who lived on the raw flesh of people originated as children who rubbed their bodies daily with dry sand until "the skin became hard and calloused like a woman's hand when the harvest was over." Accordingly, they grew to be "like men of stone," or the hard giants who "swept down upon the scattered settlements of the five nations," mutilating or devouring the bodies of men, women, and children until they were subdued by the "Good Ruler" who "saw that men would become exterminated unless he intervened" (Parker: 1923, pp. 394–95). Those creatures thus originate with recognizably human features and easy to imagine reflexes before they become superhuman monsters subdued only by a greater-than-human godlike figure.

To cite another example, a passage from the Navajo creation story describes the Holy People (*Haashch'ééh din'é*) as creatures "who could perform magic," who "could travel swiftly and . . . travel far," who "know how to ride the sunbeam and the light ray . . . and how to follow the path of the rainbow. They [feel] no pain, and nothing in any world could change the way they [are]." But they likewise possess human intelligence along with other recognizably human qualities (Zolbrod: 1984, pp. 58, 352 n. 13). The four holy chiefs express an anger like that which humans exhibit when they expel the squabbling air spirit people from an otherwise balanced world (Zolbrod: 1984, pp. 370–39). And *Haashch'ééltí'í* the Talking God together with his companion *Tó neinilí* the Water God show the glee of grandparents at the birth of the warrior twins (Zolbrod: 1984, p. 183). As Luckert suggests, then, the "greater-than-human" conception of externally sacred can reflect a very human internally felt awareness.

Similarly, Beck and Waters assert that "*sacred* means something special, something out of the ordinary," and yet something "very personal" to "each one of us because it describes our dreams, our changing, and our personal way of seeing the world." But, they add, the sacred is "also something that is shared"—a "collective experience . . . necessary in order to keep the oral traditions and sacred ways vital" (Beck, Waters, and Francisco, p. 6). Among the Objibwe it is outward appearance that humans and greater-than-humans share. What differentiates them, however, is power, whose "realization comes in a being's or object's ability to transform itself into another shape" (Ghezzi, p. 45). The starting point, however, is the human form in its manifest shape common to people and spirits alike prior to any metamorphosis the latter may undergo. Whatever it is, then, the sacred helps to define a community by linking it with something beyond itself in space, time, and natural limits, while simultaneously connecting it with what exists naturally and can be observed within spatial or temporal limits.

That connection of the transcendent and the natural can be seen in Arthur C. Parker's list of "Basic Premises" underlying the Seneca narratives he compiles, for example, as well as in the Iroquois poetry discussed in Chapter Two below. The "unseen spirits" in Seneca lore that "pervade all nature and affect man for good or evil" must be placated by the things that people actually do rather than by magic or superhuman deeds (1923, p. 3); animals are said to have souls, but they "are alike in their nature to the souls of human beings (p. 4); when a person dreams while asleep, the soul leaves the body, guided by a "dream god" from another world dispatched to direct the dreamer's actions in this one (pp. 4–5). In such ways do humans interact with nonhumans or the creatures in this world interrelate with spirits from some other.

Accordingly, poetry acquires the power to connect the inner self and the natural with what dwells outside the self and beyond nature. In one respect or another, that potential resides in the verbal expression of all cultures, although some may recognize the presence of the sacred more consciously than others. The limits of what dwells external to the self or to what is observable may be quite differently fixed in oral traditions that acknowledge the greater-than-human reality more directly than modern Europe's written poetry might conceptualize it. The people of San Juan Pueblo might jointly envision life-giving rain as the product of spirit beings, for example, summoned from distant lakes that dispatch them first as clouds before they materialize as kachinas (see Laski). In Stephen Crane's "The Blue Hotel," however, snow is merely an observable condition of mechanical indifference requiring no explanation as a seemingly innocent card game ends in a needless death—explicable in terms of how humans manifestly behave. Sacred poetry therein can range more widely outside the domain of the verifiably accountable than conventional secular literature, especially in a Native American setting where natural forces such as wind's power and the sun's energy can assume supernatural dimensions. In Navajo storytelling and ceremonial drama, for example, *Nilch'i* the Wind and *Jóhonaa'éí* the Sun, respectively, whisper special instructions to selected protagonists and function as a warrior or procreator of warriors as well as a life-giving force for plants (see Zolbrod: 1984, pp. 184–87, for example).

Such overlapping of the real with the supernatural can also be seen in the older poetry of Europe and England that antedates the advent of print among certain communities. The medieval lyrics and early ballads that survive only as printed works in literary textbooks offer but one set of examples. In "The Corpus Christi Carol," a falcon bears a young man to a velvet-lined chamber lying in a secluded brown forest wherein a maiden perpetually keeps vigil over an eternally bleeding knight. In the traditional ballad, "The Three Ravens," birds of prey speak like humans while a pregnant doe kisses the wounds of a youth wounded in battle. And in "The Wife of Usher's Well," three drowned youths

return from the dead on Martinmas to have supper with their
mother. In such cases, enduring echoes of an older "pagan" notion of the sacred resemble those that resonate actively in ongoing
Native American oral traditions.

Because these works are stored only by way of print, however,
readers overlook their origins as oral poems once produced in
tribal or tribelike communities. Once their origins are fully acknowledged, those poems can be amplified by today's surviving
tribal works in ways that conventional literary exegesis does not
easily permit. Sacred preliterate poetry allows the externalization
of what is internal on a scale not always expected in mainstream
written poetry. It permits the exchange with others of an interior
awareness at once deeply felt and "greater-than-human." With
stylized force it verbalizes that grasp of the real among members
of a community, whether that reality is human or transcendent.
Thus, oral poetry functions in a special everyday way to place the
sacred in a cultural context.

Orally transmitted verbal artifacts thereby combine to express
a culture's full conception of the sacred by articulating the place of
this world in a larger cosmic scheme; they define relationships
among human groups; and they likewise define connections between human beings and other creatures, whether the animals
who share the earth's products or the supernaturals who preside
over them. In a variety of styles employing a wide range of
themes and incorporating a panoply of ideas and observations,
those orally composed and recited poems identify the origins of
the earth and its manifest features, of the organisms that populate
it, and of the people dwelling thereon. They likewise dwell on
abiding relationships between the shaping forces of a once soft,
malleable cosmos and the creatures shaped as it hardened. As Ortiz says of the "Tewa myth of origin," those people specify perceptions of a dynamic two-way relationship between "human and
spiritual existence" while organizing nothing less than "time and
space within the geographical area they consider their world"
(Ortiz, p. 9).

Because they suggest alternative views of the sacred, works of
oral poetry in many cases also distinguish between mythic time

(what the Zunis call the *inoote*) and remembered time; and therein they designate relationships between the phenomenal and the supernatural as neither conventional history nor empirical investigation can specify.[4] Where applicable, they serve to predicate historic movements and events the way the Pentateuch fuels Zionism and the Gospels once prompted the Crusades. By their very nature, they call for a special kind of language distinct from the way it is used in ordinary, everyday discourse. All of that contributes what is most basic to a culture's verbal identity. Thus, in my judgement, sacred poetry remains fundamental to any society and does so in a special way when orally transmitted—all of which reinforces the need to recognize the traditional poetic activity of Native American peoples.

Ethnographers often seek to demonstrate the close relationship between sacred texts and the workings of everyday life in a given culture. Ortiz provides one noteworthy example, where he specifically summarizes the "myth of origin and the early migrations of the Tewa" and goes on to explain how in the context of that narrative "the Tewa conceptualize and classify their social, spiritual, and physical world today" and "make [the story] meaningful in behavioral terms" (p. 13). Missing from such discussions, however, is the application of *poesis* in them. By that term I mean an awareness of poetic qualities in how the story was created, stored, and maintained in its application to ordinary and ceremonial life.

I can see how the objection might be made that in our own secular culture here in the United States, sacred texts might be growing increasingly unimportant. Schoolchildren no longer participate in what was once called "morning devotions," where a passage from Scriptures was customarily read along with a recitation of "The Lord's Prayer." Court decisions have been made to restrain municipalities from displaying nativity scenes in public places. Some would believe that with the demise of Protestant hegemony in the United States the sacred no longer plays the central role here that it once played, so that our sacred texts have lost the centrality that I maintain has a place in every culture. And from there it becomes all too easy to presume limitations in how broadly the sacred applies to poetry everywhere.

I think I could argue against that point two ways, however. First, the Bible has remained so fundamental to the advance of European culture that its formative impact will survive any degree of secularization; its sacred influence is etched in Western consciousness with or without continued recognition. The worst that could happen would be for us to forget the Bible's historical thrust—which would be a pity, in my view. Second, the Judeo-Christian West may very well define the sacred too narrowly, inclined as it is to associate it exclusively with Scriptures, just as it tends to limit the presence of poetry to verse compositions generally consigned to schoolbooks, college anthologies, or glossy periodicals. The trick is to move poetry off the printed page; then expand the meaning of the word *sacred* beyond the Bible's parameters and thus not limit it exclusively to Judeo-Christian conceptions of the "greater-than-human reality" of which Luckert speaks in his effort to define religion (1976, p. 5). Indeed, a secularized Western culture has its sacred texts, too. They range from the "self-evident truths" cited in the Declaration of Independence to Jonathan Swift's "Sweetness and Light," or Matthew Arnold's "best that has been thought and said"; or from Kant's Categorical Imperative to Thomas Carlyle's vision of history as "the first distinct product of man's spiritual nature" and "his earliest expression of what can be called Thought" (p. 80), to Ralph Waldo Emerson's Oversoul. Those concepts, too, appeal to "greater-than-human reality configurations"; they too can stimulate the most intense poetic creativity.

Located beyond the constricting boundaries of Western literature, North America's tribal cultures may demonstrate even more clearly how conceptions of the sacred govern poetry-making, which in turn impacts on people's lives in a general way. John Farella, who illustrates that point superbly in *The Wind in a Jar*, uses ancient narratives to find meaning in everyday events among contemporary Navajos caught in the crossfire between orally transmitted values internal to tribal life and the modern world's alien world view. The old stories, he writes, "provide a template, a standard, through which [Navajo] lives . . . can be ordered and understood," and in every instance those stories tell of encounters with a "greater-than-human-reality configuration" (Farella, p. 130). Indeed, poetry and the sacred converge more commonly in day-to-day affairs than current print-based conceptions seem to indicate in mainstream Western cultures. Or so I wish to suggest by explaining how the Native American voice can be read when encountered on the printed page.

Sacred Texts and
Iroquois Culture
~ *A Case Study*

FROM A MIXED body of textual translations of poetry originally
recited, four Iroquois works show how alternate conceptions of
the sacred can nourish nonliterary poetic activity, and how the resulting poetry helps maintain the culture that has produced it. As
Zumthor says in his study of oral poetry throughout the "Old
World," "Ideally pure orality defines a civilization of 'live' voice,
where it grounds a dynamism, at once both guardian of the values
of speech and creator of the forms of discourse needed to maintain
social cohesion and group morality" (p. 26).

Such a suggestion invites an examination of a community's
formalized oral discourse to determine if indeed it expresses a
shared morality and shapes activity according to a common out-
look. When assembled in printed form, the Seneca works I wish to
discuss provide a body of poetry ample enough to initiate such an
inquiry. They include a creation narrative more or less accepted
by the confederated Iroquois tribes; a ceremonial prayer of thanks
common to them all; an account of how the original five tribes
formed a confederacy; and a written version of the condolence ritual that serves to perpetuate that union. At the risk of repeating
what is widely known, let me add that the confederacy includes
five original Algonquin tribes including the Seneca, the Onondaga, the Mohawk, the Cayuga, and the Oneida—plus the Tus-
carora, who joined later. Although the original five once made war

on each other, even then they shared key cultural traits, as the texts indicate; but as poetry those works also functioned to draw the five tribes into a tightly unified single cultural system.

The Story of Creation

APPARENTLY THE FIVE nations shared a common creation story prior to confederation and thus maintained pretty much the same sacred vision. Usually referred to simply as the Iroquoian cosmology, that account is also called by folklorists "The Woman Who Fell from the Sky."[1] Most effective in Hewitt's written English version, it is the first of the four texts I think of as combining to preserve in writing the religiopoetic underpinnings of Iroquoian culture. No available translation seems to reflect its poetic texture at the surface, at least at first—especially since it is printed in prose form rather than as verse. In what it relates, however, the narrative bespeaks a deep artistry in much the same way that elements of narrative art can survive a pedestrian translation of Homer or *Beowulf*, or the way that an aesthetic presence is apprehended in an artistic work in any material medium, whether an imprint on a cave wall, a pediment on an ancient Greek temple, or a necklace of turquoise and abalone. Combining male-female conflict with accounts of cosmic creation and good brother–bad brother contention, it invites comparison with some of the world's great literary works. It too plumbs the human psyche in confrontation with the pervasive riddles of life and death, creation and destruction, or good and evil that crave articulation across all cultural and linguistic barriers. Even when crudely translated as data and without the slightest attempt to observe or replicate any kind of poetic texture, the story has a capacity for arousing literary taste. Thus it offers a rationale for exploring the possibility that a tribal people like the Senecas can produce poetry in a preliterate setting.

The story features a pivotal struggle between a prototypical man and wife on a par with the Genesis account of Adam and Eve or Hesiod's account of Pandora; it includes a counterpart to a divine conception equivalent to that of the New Testament Gospels or such descriptions of divine procreation among humans as Ovid records in *The Metamorphoses*. It describes the creation of the earth's plants and animals along with the making of those mortals who eventually are to populate that world and maintain it; and it includes something of a deadly struggle for control of the world by two brothers, one good and one evil. Something about it compels appeal even in the crudest, most prosaic retellings, either orally or in print.

On the conceptual level I consider narratives of that sort to be deeply poetic; for they envision communication and communion between the human and the greater-than-human in an effort to explain such mysteries as cosmic genesis, the origin of life on earth, and the likelihood of spiritual transmigration to another world following corporeal death. Almost inevitably composed in some preliterate form prior to being recorded by way of print, and in some cases venerated as the Bible is by Christians, they represent human speculation so heightened that it demands special expression to be stored in the collective memory long before any such technology permits them to be stored alphabetically. It is too easy to dismiss such accounts as myth—a term so deadeningly familiar and widely ill applied that I shall try to avoid using it—and to think no more about the imaginative artistry fundamental to their creation. But they reside at the center of the universally applied art of poetry-making throughout the human community.

"The Woman Who Fell from the Sky" takes place in an ancient time before the world acquired its present hardened shape. Essentially, it tells how Tharonhiawagon or Sky-Holder casts his spouse Mature Flower from a preternatural domain in the sky to the bottom of a large lake here on earth, out of a mistaken belief that she has been impregnated by a rival male. There, she lands on the back of a turtle who gently lifts her to the water's surface, expanding as it emerges until it is transformed into a vast island. Whereupon she gives birth to a daughter who, in turn, bears two sons sired by the wind—the benign, creative Good Mind and his destructive, evil twin, Warty One. When fully grown, the second tries to interfere as the first contrives with his grandmother to give the earth its contours of hills and rivers and to populate it with grasses and shrubs and trees, with fish and animals and birds, and finally with human beings, and then to fill the skies with sun and moon, with stars, and with the sacred winds.

The Thank-You Prayer

A SECOND TEXT—the thanksgiving prayer—reiterates in concentrated form the subsequent Iroquois conception of time and space. In all likelihood, it too predates confederation. Yet to this day it is still uniformly recited from tribe to tribe to introduce and conclude some dozen and a half yearly longhouse ritual gathering events—all timed according to the position of the Pleiades. The major ones include the midwinter new year and maple ceremonies, the spring seed-planting and strawberry ceremonies, the little corn and green corn summer ceremonies, and the dry corn and harvest ceremonies of fall (see Foster, pp. 109–34). Especially in Richard Johnny John's translation of a Seneca version, the prayer makes for an important text that allows the careful reader a close glimpse of an Iroquois greater-than-human reality (see Rothenberg, pp. 4–11, 347).[2] Chanted by an elder to open and close a longhouse ceremony, it summarizes the creation by reviewing how Good Mind made a world replete with plants, animals, and humans dynamically balanced against an equally well-arranged celestial domain full of spirits and stellar bodies. That conception feeds into a code of ideal behavior: the speaker bids all members of the assembly to greet each other and to remain aware of the vision of a greater-than-human reality that all must share and help to maintain. Here, too, a deep poetic artistry resides in the poem. Implicitly but with an obvious spatial arrangement of plants by their proximity to the earth's surface, animals by how they move, and celestial objects by their function and where they dwell in the sky, the poem classifies all known objects and spirits for the celebrants assembled in their longhouse gathering place. With each stanza, focus progresses from closely terrestrial items like water, grass, and shrubs through living creatures ranked by size, and on to celestial elements ranked according to their distance from the earth, thus completing a vision that attains a viable greater-than-human reality on poetic terms (see Zolbrod: 1992a).

The Dekanawida Myth

AS A THIRD religiopoetic item, the individual Iroquois nations also share an account of how the mythic hero Dekanawida mediates between the tribes and forges a lasting peace among them. Bearing in its most comprehensive written form the title *The Constitution of the Five Nations or the Iroquois Book of the Great Law*, it divides loosely into a narrative part combined with an expository portion.[3] Much of its deeply intrinsic poetic quality emerges through its theme of compassionate bereavement, which intensifies as the tale progresses and provides an underlying explanation for the murderous warfare that once bitterly divided the individual tribes. The conflict between them brings mounting enmity, and as the killing continues sorrow mounts and becomes an unrelenting need for vengeance—until the Huron visionary Dekanawida crosses Lake Ontario into Iroquois country on his mission for peace. There he finds the grieving Mohawk Hayenwatha, whose unmitigated grief over the death of his wife and daughters has driven him into angry exile and insane paralysis (Parker: 1916, pp. 18–24, 114). When Dekanawida encounters this solitary mourner, he offers him the comfort of condolence, which cures him of his crazed bereavement, and thereafter they resolve to work together to spread the gospel of mitigating grief by mutual condolence among the five tribes.

The unifying theme of their shared grief carries over into the expository part of the text through the poetic use of symbols along with a special way of verbalizing individual and intertribal relationships. That portion describes how the Iroquois nations are to conjoin as five tribes "of equal standing and of equal power" (p. 103) who pledge to grieve in unison for the deceased members of any particular one. Basically, it is that universal willingness now to share grief where it had once been callously ignored which forges a cohesive political body, matching the cohesiveness of earth and sky as described in the thankgiving prayer. Its unity is represented by such symbols as "four great, long white roots" of a single tree which "shall shoot forth" in the four cardinal directions"; as the tree's trunk and branches which shall be seen perpetually and accepted by all of "the nations of the earth"; and as a circle formed when members of the Five Confederate Nations "bind ourselves together by taking hold of each other's hands," and strong enough "so that if a tree shall fall prostrate upon it, it could neither shake nor break it" (p. 102).

Although the *Constitution of the Five Nations* lacks the immediate poetic texture found in Richard Johnny John's expertly textured English version of the "Thank-You Prayer," it displays subtextual poetic qualities like narrative and thematic unity which transcend unpoetically written translations. Even if we lack access to the textured performance in a Seneca language, and thus cannot take measure of the surface poetry in a given recitation, much of its deep poetic force can surmount the verbal displacement of being printed in some other language. The copious symbolic and metaphorical expression in Parker's version of Dekanawida's Great Law, for example, far surpasses the droning remoteness of today's legal prose, thanks to its reference to roots extending from the sky world deep into earthly soil, spreading the "great power of long vision" (p. 101); or its description of the uniting confederate lords "taking hold of each other's hands firmly and forming a circle so strong that if a tree shall fall prostrate upon it, it could neither shake nor break it" (p. 102). While not always easy to recognize and sometimes too abstract in and of themselves, those features are essential to poetry.

When the surface properties of poetry exist without such internally resonating conceptions, an empty display of texture results in vapid doggerel. We see that phenomenon in standard greeting cards and hear it in some (but by no means all) song lyrics. On the other hand, a deeply resident poetic conception can surmount the absence of verbal gloss. In the story of Dekanawida, the quality of deep poetry originates with the repeated idea that war is essentially the wanton, unreasoning destruction of life without accompanying regret and with no effort to achieve and maintain civic harmony. Such things as clashing beliefs or conflicting ideologies merely allow warring parties to rationalize slaughter and prevent them from forging common bonds. The tribes grow "callous and so accustomed to troubled times that they did not care for the sorrows of others and even despised the tears of mourners" (Parker: 1916, p. 114). That defiance of true reason and compassion is reinforced poetically in the narrative portion of the *Constitution* by descriptions of Atoharto, the chief perpetrator of the warfare among the five nations. He is described in one account as having "snakes in his hair and covering his shoulders and one great one came up from his thighs and went over his shoulders" (Parker, p. 115). In another, he is called an evil wizard with "a twisted body and a twisted mind," whose hair "was a mass of tangled snakes" and who "killed and devoured all men who approached him uninvited" (Paul A. W. Wallace, p. 18). Such descriptions take on the metaphorical quality that marks the poet's way of conceptualizing relationships so as to command thought and attention with highlighted expression.

Together, then, the narrative and expository portions of the Parker text employ the deeper devices and techniques of poetry to articulate the terms of what might be called a "greater-than-human" society—a society or a community greater than any one individual in it, wherein the value of an individual life is recognized by the single tribe, wherein the smaller tribal unit is valued by the larger confederacy, and wherein that broader collectivity is unified by broadly shared symbols and a common metaphorical perception articulated through language deeply poetic rather than only superficially so. In that large polity, myth and vision combine to formulate the political underpinnings of an enduring culture sustained by poetic insight into an awareness of the greater-than-human.

The Condolence Ritual

THE FOURTH UNIFYING religiopoetic text—the Iroquois *Ritual of Condolence*—indicates how a shared "lamentation," or what Zumthor calls "one of the primordial forms of poetic discourse" (p. 74), can help an entire culture function at a crucial time. A ceremonial drama without the distinction between actors and spectators common in Euroamerican theater, it is performed when a member of the "supreme senate of fifty councilors" dies—a loss that might have exacerbated enmity between the tribes during the earlier period of ongoing warfare. Now, instead of being greeted with vicious glee or callous indifference, the death arouses condoling sympathy among the nations. For the occasion, they divide into two grand moieties transcendently personified as a bereaved brother and a condoling one who reenact, so to speak, in greater-than-human proportions Dekanawida's condolence of the mournfully crazed Hayenwatha to cure him with pity and compassion.[4] In its dramaturgy, it progresses from an opening summons bringing the two brothers together through sixteen separate scenelike articles, resulting in the investiture of a new council member to replace the lost one. That gradual movement from grief to recovery generates much the same kind of dramatic intensity found in a conventional stage play as its "plot" unfolds.

At the thematic heart of the work, in fact, lies a reiteration of the spatial design described by the Thank-You Prayer. Once embedded in the ritual, however, that design implies a progression from a narrowly internal preoccupation with one's own self-indulgent sorrow to a more fully transcendent and widely public external awareness of a greater-than-human, creator-shaped universe fully systematic in its very conception. Paralleling the shift in attention from an immediate spot progressively outward to the farthest imaginable reach of space, articles one through eight describe how the grieving patient is urged to expand his focus as he recovers, so that he can progress from his self-preoccupied suffering to regain full participation in the confederation.

Initially, he sits in deadening constraint on a husk mat in a dark lodge—blinded with his grief, deafened by it, and unable to speak and move (Bierhorst: 1974, pp. 129–36). Step by step, however, the condoling brother gently reminds him of the confederation and its foundation in the Great Law and the story of its origin. Even in translation, the poetic surface of the language serves to unfold the deeply artistic blend of memory and conceptual power that those powerful words relay. Thus the patient recovers his sight, his hearing, and his capacity for speech—finally getting him to leave the spot where he lies paralyzed and to walk out of the lodge into the sunlight where he may see first the ground in front of him, then the shrubs a little farther off, then the more distant objects and animals, and finally the celestial objects positioned farther and farther out into the sky until he can once again contemplate the vast cosmos and its presiding spirits.

In what he says to mitigate the grief of the bereaved brother, the condoling one reenacts Dekanawida's sympathetic restoration of Hayenwatha from the depths of his crazed, paralyzing grief. His words also reiterate the tight organization of the Great Law, with its detailed stipulation that grief must be removed throughout the confederacy before social harmony can be assured; that all of its tribes are of equal standing; that all members of its tribal council are likewise equal; and that power is to be distributed commensurate with the balanced distribution of all things in the cosmos originally designed and created by Mature Flower and her grandson Good Mind.

Poetry as a Cultural Institution

TAKEN TOGETHER, the four texts merge in how they unite the five tribes as a single cultural community and thus invite inquiry beyond the summary treatment I give them in this all-too-brief introductory discussion. They overlap referentially and combine to envision a world and a surrounding universe formed in some long-ago mythic time of greater-than-human creation. Yet it is also a world that defines ongoing social reality in keeping with the ceremonial activity described and perpetuated by the works. It is my clear understanding that to this day such a world is invoked directly in the longhouse at strawberry festival time or at the green corn ceremony or the midwinter ceremony, thanks to the stylized use of language and the greater-than-human conception it articulates. Commentators like Fenton and Paul Wallace verify that a great deal of Iroquois tradition survives by way of ongoing ceremonial life and of the thought and belief that it has produced.

In her summary of the "Longhouse Religion" still practiced throughout the confederacy among the various Iroquois reservations scattered across New York State and into Canada, Elisabeth Tooker explains how its concerns reflect the abiding values expressed in the four texts (1978: pp. 454–65). At the standard ceremonial gatherings, participants exchange food and tobacco to render their thanks to the various "spirit forces" described and acknowledged in the creation narrative and the story of the league's founding.

Those spirits also figure in a host of satellite narratives routinely performed and recited as part of the longhouse religion. All told, those stories could fill volumes and invite systematic investigation in their own right. They incorporate innumerable characters and themes, ranging from the mighty Sky Grabber and his resilient spouse, along with her daughter and two grandsons, to the various animals, the pigmy people, and the formidable stone giants (see, for example, Canfield; Parker, 1923). The spirits also include the original founders of the league who survive perpetually through their names, which are recited whenever a new councilor is selected to replace a deceased one whose identity he then assumes.

I have listened to recitations of the Thank-You Prayer in Seneca at the Cold Spring Longhouse near Salamanca, New York, and can attest to its impact. An essential part of every ceremonial meeting, it aligns the common view of creation with everyday life by connecting any particular gathering with the general conception of a greater-than-human existence. The longhouse ceremony is a time to share food and mutual good wishes, along with news and gossip reminiscent of the way in which deep socializing occurs after an evangelical Christian revival meeting or during the course of a big Navajo sing. People greet each other with smiles and formulaic expressions of goodwill that resonate with ancient sentiments. The longhouse also becomes a focal point for momentous special events. No decision of major magnitude made by the community can be done without invoking the prayer's vision of how the world and surrounding cosmos were created. At such gatherings standard phrases like "Now we greet each other," and "this is the way it should be in our minds"—repeated in Richard Johnny John's translation of the Thank-You Prayer—assume a poetic depth not easily manifested on paper without a reader's self-conscious awareness that print is but the silent counterpart to the speaking or singing voice.

Seneca scholar George Abrams describes, for example, how it was recited when the original Cold Spring Longhouse had to be relocated to make way for a reservoir following the erection of the

Kinzua Dam on the New York–Pennsylvania border. A bitter occasion for the Seneca nation and hence for the entire confederacy, the displacement required "the desanctification" of the old structure and a proper "dedication" of its replacement on higher ground nearby. To prepare for the move, "representatives of all Iroquois Long House communities in the United States and Canada met at the Tonawanda Reservation," on June 12, 1965, Abrams writes. The meeting included the ceremonial exchange of tobacco and its traditional burning, the formal display of appropriate wampum, and the customary sequence of speeches to mark the event. "Most moving," however, was the "chanted, regular measured verses...of the Thanksgiving Speech, enumerating the people, plants, water, trees, animals, birds, 'the three sisters' the winds, thunder, sun, moon, stars, the Four Beings, Handsome Lake, and the Creator" (Abrams, pp. 24–25). While I lack the time and space to elaborate, the ceremonial gatherings that feature the prayer remain central to the preservation of longhouse culture and the way of life that it perpetuates.

Evidently, the foregrounded poetic language used at such events functions to preserve ideals and visions still embedded in the way people behave throughout the confederacy; it maintains unity among them equivalent to the way in which it can help non-Iroquois readers to understand tribal behavior once it is committed to print. I bid others to explore that possibility more thoroughly and transform my initial generalizations and speculations into a deeper appreciation for tribal poetic practice, or to undertake a fully detailed investigation and analysis of their own. I hope that Native American scholars in particular will undertake such investigation—particularly to correct my errors and misconceptions. Eventually, their own indigenous understanding should prevail to assure that European ways of knowing are subordinated to the knowledge and principles that originate indigenously, as they inevitably must, from a vast traditional network like that of the Iroquois. No application of outside standards are required to justify the artistry and social value of a verbal performance like the Thank-You Prayer or its allied recitations. Far to the contrary, such Native poetic practice can add considerable light to how poetry in the so-called Old World actually originated and was once used—or how it may still be used, especially if we learn to recognize its presence off the page in our own everyday oral-ceremonial lives.

Something identifiably sacred resonates among the four central Iroquois texts, just as they resonate with the poetry which conveys them and the culture they define, and as the language of other tribes' poetic artifacts do, too. Where bland prose translation of them does not reflect poetic texture, it sometimes does reveal a deeper poetic structure, connecting them in a way that shows how poetry functions to define culture. Claire Farrer (pp. 33–100) has expertly detailed the same poetic connection between the *poesis* inherent in the Mescalero Apache account of cosmic creation and the way life is lived individually and ceremonially, just as I have observed such a connection between Navajo creation accounts and all phases of everyday life, both verbally and materially.

Anyone who patiently listens and watches can find similar connections in other cultures, I am now convinced, including our own. Pay attention to the cadences of Martin Luther King's "I Have a Dream" speech, with its carefully paced biblical allusions, or heed the central images in commonplace hymns like "Amazing Grace," or "Will the Circle Be Unbroken." Alfonso Ortiz asserts that the continuity between human and spiritual existence that he describes in Tewa culture is rooted in ethnographic data (p. 26), implying thereby that anthropologists can document the relationship I speak of. All well and good, but why not add texts like these to that data, too, recognizing in them fine expressions of the sacred and the poetic alike as they conjoin at gatherings intensified by song or ritualized speech? In that case, the continuity between the human and the spiritual that Ortiz speaks of—and that Luckert attempts to comprehend with the phrase "greater than human"—may exist by way of *poesis*, raising thereby the possibility that poetry and religion do indeed converge in everyday human reality, even where the so-called pagan or the secular seems to prevail.

THREE

Classifying
Poetic Texts
~ *Voice*

AT THE OUTSET, I mentioned that I would try to classify sacred Native American texts. Poetry in general, in fact, lacks an effective taxonomy, which may explain why we have trouble dealing with it—especially in a postliterate electronic age—and why the connection between poetry and the sacred or poetry and the broader culture that nourishes it remains as unclear as does the distinction between poetry and literature. If that art form whose primary medium is language can be broadly designated as the genus poetry, though, it should be possible to isolate narrower and more currently meaningful categories of it so as to understand better how examples resemble each other and how they differ, particularly when we avert the narrow print-oriented Euroamerican assumptions about what poetry is. Let me work on that possibility to see where it may lead in the effort to appreciate the sacred poetry of people like the Iroquois, the Navajo, or the Tewa of San Juan Pueblo, and to apply such verbal art to a renewed understanding of where and how poetry today serves people everywhere.

Two Kinds of Voice

IF WE ACCEPT the idea that language is the medium that sets poetry apart from other arts, we can start classifying it according to voice; and once we recognize that texts like the Seneca Thank-You poem, the Navajo *Diné bahane'*, or the San Juan Rain God Drama emerge from preliterate traditions that are no less capable of producing poetry than Homeric Greece was, we find that with or without an alphabetical technology tribal North America is as much a wellspring of poetry as Europe has been. By listening to singers and storytellers in and out of the Seneca longhouse or Navajo hogans, and by watching rituals, ceremonies, and festivals in Navajo communities and among various pueblos, I believe I have found ways to distinguish broadly between two vocal properties that suggest parallel distinctions in standard written British, European, or American literary texts. Here I merely offer the broad guidelines; further refinements remain to be recognized, which I hope others will attempt. Please remember that what I present here is only a beginning.

Loosely speaking, a Seneca or a Navajo performer can sing or chant on the one hand and speak conversationally on the other. During a period of frequent visits that I made from 1973 through 1977 to his home in upstate New York, Avery Jimerson, a shaman and a venerable Seneca musician, recited several traditional stories to me along with singing many songs. He also spoke of how in the late fifties and early sixties the people of the Allegany Seneca reservation had to move out of their valley to make room for the Kinzua Dam—a story he had obviously told before. By the time I recorded his English account I had observed in his voice and body language patterns of cadence, pitch, and syntax more loosely structured than song displays.

Since he was also a singer, I could easily spot contrasts. He usually sang accompanied by a small water drum and often moved his feet to reinforce its rhythm, for instance. He closed his eyes, and his neck tightened with the increased tension in his vocal chords. Vocables were abundant and the referential frame was often narrow. While the stories he told developed plotlike to cover a series of consecutive incidents with a certain syntactical and semantic looseness, his lyrics were tightly contained within a smaller verbal loop, so to speak; they included rigidly repetitive units of syntax that were parallel in structure and might easily be construed as individual verses. Instead of telling stories, his songs conveyed or virtually created images—the flight of a bird, the gait of a bear, a wolf running across a field. Or sometimes they pinpointed some human act, such as issuing a warning or singing off-key, often satirically or with a touch of humor (see Rothenberg for typical examples, pp. 16–41). In terms of sound, the difference was as marked as that between the way a choir sings and a preacher talks in a Protestant church.

When listened for, such contrasts can easily be heard anywhere in tribal America—or wherever singers appear in concert in contemporary popular culture, for that matter. In her fine but little-known volume of Okanagan lyrics, Eloise Streit remarked of her main informant, "The poetry of Chief Sepass has a lift at the end of the line instead of a crop common to Engish inflection"—much like what I heard when I listened to Mr. Jimerson or when I hear Navajos sing. "This upward lift is a characteristic more of music than Indian recitative, and must be considered against the background of drum accompaniment," Streit continues. "The drum sets the beat of chanted speech; the singer stands still for recitative, but dances to the livelier rhythm. He himself is the living expression of the song. The movement of his hands tells a story" (p. 108). Kinetically, a song can be more broadly dynamic, conveying the visual contrast between someone fairly stationary and someone in full motion. Observe the movement of a popular singer performing on tv, for example, or in concert. Meanwhile, in terms of content and linear development, the difference between a song and a story can be as great as that between a snapshot or a single frame and an entire film. Lyrics that are sung a cappella or to instrumental accompaniment differ so manifestly from verse arrayed on a silent page that listeners in print cultures consider them as music but do not associate them with poetry.

I am surprised that scholars and literary critics have not explored the relationship between those two arts more than they have. Of the few who have made the connection, Franz Boas is among the first in the modern era (see also Booth). He was an anthropologist rather than a critic, and today's readers will want to monitor his repeated use of the term *primitive* with caution. His observations still largely apply, however, and continue to await further exploration. In invoking lyricism, of course, I open up the proverbial can of worms, since lyric poetry has been so broadly and variously defined. The term was once used in recognition of a close association between music and poetry. After the European Renaissance, however, "the link between poetry and music was gradually broken, and the term 'lyric' came to be applied to short poems expressive of a poet's thought and feeling" (Drabble, p. 596). Along with that associative shift came a wider semantic loosening wherein the term *poetry* came more and more to designate emotionally intense thought and feeling. Thereby Wordsworth's famous definition of poetry as "the spontaneous overflow of powerful feelings" very likely led to the commonplace blurring of lyric poetry with printed verse, whether metrical, blank, or free, and to the rather haphazard generalization that poetry and verse are one and the same while alternative genres such as drama and prose narrative are complementary species of literature, which is tacitly assumed always to be written. Standard textbook guides to literature usually reflect such a view, and they have not yet fully recognized the importance of modern electronic transmission in the changing conception of poetry.[1]

Boas points out that "the two fundamental forms, song and tale, are found among all the people of the world and must be considered the primary forms of literary activity." He then goes on to observe "that primitive poetry does not occur without music, and that it is frequently accompanied by expressive motions or by dance." And he points out that "an important difference between modern and primitive prose" is that the former "is largely determined by the fact that it is read, not spoken," while the latter "is based on the art of oral delivery and is, therefore, more closely related to modern oratory than to . . . printed literary style," resulting in a considerable "difference between the two forms" (p. 491).

Mark Booth is concerned primarily with European lyrics in *The Experience of Songs;* on the other hand, he makes some observations that seem to apply to Native American lyric texts, too. Moreover, he invites a careful comparison of Native American song with songs from mainstream Euroamerican cultures and with texts of standard lyric poems. "Song," he says, "gives access to a state of experience. . . . Not much change can be introduced," which makes a lyric referentially static. Its language does not so much explore or move thought forward as it expresses the fixed, accepted results of such thought or exploration having "moved forward" antecedent to the situation that the lyrics now describe (p. 24).

Citing C. M. Bowra, Booth adds that lines of pure lyric poetry are more or less "independent units" at least syntactically, sometimes almost interchangeable, and very often parallel in their structure (p. 25). All of this combines, he suggests, to invite members of the audience "to pause from their personal selves to enter into a common consciousness," admitting them "to the same participation" in a reality broadly shared (p. 26). In other words, he suggests that lyric poetry has an innate capacity to beckon listeners into a greater-than-human reality, or at least a reality greater than oneself. That possibility applies even in a secular culture, such as ours has become. Consider the popular fascination with a modern-day electronic lyric poet like Leonard Cohen and his contemporary followers. Or consider the way an entire audience will clap and sway in unison at a concert. Consider, too, the lyrics of certain tv commercials, especially those for soft drinks like Coke and Pepsi.

In its purest form, lyric poetry combines with instrumental music and even dance, utilizing melody and movement as it merges with sister arts. Within the framework of our own pop culture lyric poetry abounds, and besides the familiar writer-poets recognized in schools and college classrooms, we have noteworthy electronic lyricists like Kenny Rogers or Sting, among numerous others, and such now-redoubtable "classic" recording artists as Bob Dylan, John Lennon, Jim Morrison, or Mick Jagger. Their lyrics at least deserve consideration as a source of lyric poetry—some noteworthy and some not, as with the works of conventional alphabetical poets.

On the Navajo reservation, meanwhile, or at places like Jemez Pueblo or Santo Domingo in northern New Mexico, lyric poetry is a mainstay, as anyone might well realize who has witnessed or participated in a Navajo moccasin game or attended a Blessingway ceremony or a corn dance. It is commonplace to associate lyrical poetry with intense feelings—or, to put it less simplistically, with a "poetic sensibility as evidenced in a fusion of conception and image" (Preminger et al., p. 462; see also Welsh).[2] That tendency, however, has evolved for the most part in a print-oriented literary culture that has moved insidiously away from poetry's ultimate roots in speech and song, especially as literature becomes more narrowly confined to an academic subculture as a scholarly subject increasingly partitioned from mainstream society.

Colloquial poetry at its best can be just as evocative as lyrical poetry is, and can exhibit as much emotional intensity. But that evoked force seems to develop differently in a colloquial poem, especially when it is a narrative. Awaiting explanation is the way a less tightly patterned conversational declaration can arouse the alacrity a stylized lyric can evoke—how a commensurate intensity can occur in a longer, more naturally conversational narrative. It may well be that while a tightly structured lyric simply asserts the static outcome of a prior action, a story builds its dialectic more gradually by describing that action's progress. "The Lord is my shepherd, I shall not want," begins the Twenty-third Psalm in the arrestingly lyrical idiom of the King James Bible; "He maketh me to lie down in green pastures—" as if an undisclosed ordeal leading to that conclusion is now over and nothing else remains to be expressed but the psalm's intense outcry. Or as Sitting Bull—who was highly regarded for the artistry of his lyrics—sang after his long ordeal prior to surrendering:

> A warrior
> I have been
> Now!
> It is all over
> A hard time
> I have
> (Densmore, p. 284; repr. Astrov, p. 127)

On the other hand, a growing intensity might accompany a more loosely colloquial account of something like Christian's harrowing "walk through the valley of the shadow" in John Bunyan's *Pilgrim's Progress*—which I can easily posit as a narrative leading to such a statement.

Unlike lyrics, colloquial poems tend to acquire intensity gradually, especially when they tell stories. What compels us to continue reading a Tony Hillerman novel, or one by Dickens? we need to ask, while audiences expect to be immediately enraptured by a song by Kathy Mattea or Tracy Chapman. The lyric voice and the colloquial voice may produce comparable effects in the long run, but they do so in contrasting ways. Consider how suspense slowly builds and is subsequently sustained in the *Night Chant* narrative that Washington Matthews includes in his description of that ceremony. "Many years ago, in the neighborhood of Dzilna'oodilii, in the Carrizo Mountains, dwelt a family of six: the father, the mother, two sons, and two daughters," it begins in a rambling colloquial style (Matthews: 1897; repr., 1993, p. 387). It then goes on to tell the story of a warrior's capture and near-fatal escape from an enemy tribe. By contrast, notice the impression of intense relief quickly evident in the chantway's final morning song—evident even in translation. Chanted over the patient to terminate his ritual ordeal as the protagonist's long-suffering surrogate, the lyric assures that respite is now at hand in a world whose lost harmony has been restored with the divine help:

> Lullaby, lullaby,
> It is daybreak. Lullaby.
> Now comes the Daylight Boy.
> Lullaby, lullaby,
> Now it is day. Lullaby.
> Now comes the Daylight Girl.
> Lullaby, lullaby.
> (Matthews: 1897, p. 463)

Between them, the slow-to-develop narrative and the swiftly arresting song mark the extremes of the naturally conversational colloquial voice and the finely stylized voice of pure song.

I would like to enter the suggestion that all poetic artifacts can be located somewhere on a voice continuum between the lyrical extreme of song and the colloquial extreme of ordinary conversation—or what generally is transformed to become prose on the written page. Hence in mainstream European manuscript tradition lyric poetry exists, on the one hand, not only in the songs and sonnets of Shakespeare or the written verse of old standbys like Wyatt, Surrey, and Sidney, but in hymns, choral music, and opera, along with printed material salvaged in one form or another from the unlettered so-called folk or peasant cultures of Europe. It even exists in today's emerging postliterate, electronic tradition of radio, recordings, and video through the lyrics of pop and rock. At the other extreme, colloquial poetry resides more prosaically in novels or short stories, together with essays and dialogue in movies or threatrical plays.

I would even argue that it exists in certain kinds of oratory such as sermons or well-crafted political speeches which overlap with rhetoric. Martin Luther King's "I Have a Dream" speech provides an example, as does Chief Joseph's much-quoted surrender speech (see Astrov, p. 87, or Spinden: 1908, p. 243). Passages from the former readily lend themselves to a verselike arrangement when reprinted on the page in the way that Trimmer and Hairston allow (p. 461):

I have a dream that one day this nation will rise up and live out the true meaning of its creed: "We hold these truths to be self-evident; that all men are created equal."

I have a dream that one day on the red hills of Georgia the sons of former slaves and the sons of former slaveowners will be able to sit down together at the table of brotherhood.

I have a dream that the state of Mississippi, a desert state sweltering with the heat of injustice and oppression, will be transformed into an oasis of freedom and justice.

I have a dream that my four little children will one day live in a nation where they will not be judged by the color of their skin but by the content of their character.

I have a dream today.

Its lyric qualities might become more apparent with further reduction of paragraph-like units, such as the above, to smaller linear units that help make such lyrical or semilyrical elements as repetition and parallel structure more visibly poetic:

I have a dream today.
I have a dream that one day every valley shall be exalted,
Every hill and mountain shall be made low,
The rough places will be made plain,
And the crooked places will be made straight,
And the glory of the Lord shall be revealed,
And all flesh shall see it together.

Meanwhile, Chief Joseph's speech is conventionally aligned margin to margin on the printed page, as if it were prose:

I am tired of fighting. Our chiefs are killed. Looking Glass is dead. Toohuylhulsote is dead. The old men are all dead. It is the young men who say no and yes. He who led the young men is dead. It is cold and we have no blankets. The little children are freezing to death. My people, some of them, have run away to the hills and have no blankets, no food. No one knows where they are—perhaps they are freezing to death. I want to have time to look for my children and see how many of them I can find. Maybe I shall find them among the dead. Hear me, my chiefs, I am tired. My heart is sad and sick. From where the sun now stands I will fight no more forever.

However, that compelling statement would also look and sound more like a lyric if it were written otherwise; or at least a more contrived graphic arrangement would prompt a reader to think of it in terms of voice rather than print:

I am tired of fighting.
Our chiefs are killed.
Looking Glass is dead.
Toohulhulsote is dead.
The old men are all dead.
It is the young men who say no and yes. . . .

Hear me my chiefs,
I am tired.
My heart is sad and sick.

From where the sun now stands
I will fight no more
Forever.

The numerous anecdotes that I have heard Navajos repeat might also suggest a lyric quality of voice if they were printed more deliberately than ordinary prose typesetting allows. Ready-made stories whose minor details can be adjusted extemporaneously to fit the occasion, they are customarily recited at gatherings such as banquets and council meetings. Or they are incorporated into the elaborate greetings exchanged as relatives and close friends assemble before going inside a hogan for a nightlong ceremony, or when a family member is welcomed back home after a long absence. Unfortunately, the various printed accounts of anecdotes or narratives acquired by early field-workers among Native American tribes like those compiled by Spier and Boas, and then included in anthologies such as Astrov's (pp. 267, 285, and 286, respectively), were rendered on the page colloquially. Those who first performed them may have recited them in spoken English rather than as song; or else the editors and scribes who produced either the translations or the transcriptions might have ignored any lyrical qualities evident in the original or have chosen not to try replicating them verselike on the page.

A fairly wide range of choice is open to the scribe. Paragraphs and paragraph-like units can be longer or shorter. In *Diné buhune'*, the Navajo story cycle I rendered in English, I selected small units that frequently contained carefully constructed sentences often parallel to one another and full of repetitions and finely chiseled configurations of syntax (see Zolbrod: 1984; by contrast, see Parker: 1923, where the text reflects the freer, more casually constructed language of Seneca storytelling). I did so after hours and hours of listening to singers and storytellers over many years and of observing body language, which helps to mark the difference between narrative and lyric voice in some interesting ways. Especially in the ceremonial hogan, a singer, for example, will sit almost rigidly immobilized as he chants, producing strong rhythm almost exclusively with his voice. With one foot or another, depending upon how he sits, or with a rattle, his hand, or even a finger, he may beat out a rhythm or tap. Otherwise, the body remains virtually motionless. A storyteller, on the other hand, may move the body more freely, shifting from the waist to incline forward or look from side to side, sometimes even getting up when seated or moving back and forth if standing, working hands and feet more dynamically, and turning the head while shifting eye contact. Meanwhile, the fixed vocal patterns so evident in song and chant are missing, to be replaced by a more loosely arrayed string of gestures or mannerisms which often recur in broad patterns that can be detected but that the storyteller claims not to be aware of. All of that, I contend, can be reflected in the way language is aligned on the page; just as there are shades of difference between lyric and colloquial voice, differential shadings between the fixed metrical line common to conventional verse, on the one hand, and the free, seemingly more formless prose line likewise possible on the other. The trick in transforming spoken poetry, whether lyrical or colloquial, from performance to text is to notice how speech and body language are syncopated to arrive at some accurate degree of lyric or colloquial and then to adjust the printed units accordingly.

When it comes to voice, a poem may stand at any point along the continuum to represent sound more or less lyrical or colloquial. In mainstream British literary tradition, for example, poets like John Donne or Robert Browning superimpose upon strictly measured verbal units of rhyme and meter complexities of syntax more characteristic of ordinary conversation. Those complexities materialize in conventionally printed form as run-on lines wherein linear units and units of syntax virtually clash. The result is a subdued lyricism, where rhyme and meter occur in counterpoint with non-parallel sentence structure, irregularly placed subordinate clauses, lines of various length, and seemingly unmetrical patterns of sound that help simulate ordinary speech. For instance, consider a passage like this one from John Donne's "The Funeral":

> Whoever comes to shroud me, do not harm
>   Nor question much
> That subtle wreath of hair, which crowns my arm;

> The mystery, the sign you must not touch,
> > For 'tis my outward soul,
> Viceroy to that, which then to heaven being gone,
> > Will leave this to control,
> And keep these limbs, her provinces, from dissolution.

Here, the straightforward lyrical effects that result from rhyme, strong meter, and successive lines of fixed length and relatively parallel syntax do not initially seem to occur, even where there is indeed rhyme and a fairly steady meter, however disguised or seemingly disturbed. The effect thus becomes somewhat more colloquial even where lyrical techniques are applied.

Browning likewise blends the lyrical and the colloquial so that the two seem to merge somewhere on the voice continuum between the two pure extremes, as with a passage such as this one from "My Last Duchess," where the run-on lines with their more conversational cadences all but neutralize the effects of unrelenting couplets:

> That's my last duchess painted on the wall,
> Looking as if she were alive. I call
> That piece a wonder, now: Frà Pandolf's hands
> Worked busily a day, and there she stands.
> Will't please you sit and look at her? I said
> "Frà Pandolf" by design, for never read
> Strangers like you that pictured countenance,
> The depth and passion of its earnest glance,
> But to myself they turned...

Customarily referred to as "dramatic monologs" by literary scholars, such poems become richer when thought of in terms of actual speech and more interesting still if seen as experiments by writers deliberate in the application of voice to the medium of print.

Likewise, novelists sometimes build into a colloquial prose matrix a steadily cadenced discourse that thus takes on lyrical properties to coax the text away from the pure extreme of the conversational or colloquial voice. Consider a passage such as this one by Mark Twain, from the opening paragraph of chapter XIX in *Huckleberry Finn*, that all but sings out:

> Not a sound anywheres—perfectly still—just like the whole world was asleep, only sometimes the bull-frogs a-cluttering, maybe. The first thing to see, looking away over the water, was a kind of dull line—that was the woods on t'other side—you couldn't make nothing else out; then a pale place in the sky; then more paleness, spreading around; then the river softened up, away off, and warn't black any more, but gray; you could see little dark spots drifting along, ever so far away—trading scows, and such things; and long black streaks—rafts; sometimes you could hear a sweep screaking; or jumbled up voices, it was so still, and sounds come so far; and by-and-by you could see a streak on the water which you know by the look of the streak that there's a snag there in a swift current which breaks on it and makes that streak look that way; and you see the mist curl up off of the water, and the east reddens up, and the river, and you make out a log cabin in the edge of the woods, away on the bank on t'other side of the river, being a wood-yard, likely, and piled by them cheats so you can throw a dog through it anywheres; then the nice breeze springs up, and comes fanning you from over there, so cool and fresh, and sweet to smell, on account of the woods and the flowers; . . .

By sustaining a cadence while constructing sentences that are closely parallel, Navajo storytellers I have heard create a similar effect orally, as do Seneca performers I have listened to; and Dennis Tedlock reports having heard Zunis do much the same thing. In fact, my experience as a listener has made me all the more attentive to the way literary poets can project the voice through writing. Earlier in the twentieth century, a modernist poet like T. S. Eliot moved back and forth from metered to free verse in a single work, as in "Burnt Norton" in *Four Quartets*, oscillating between highly lyrical and flatly colloquial (see Eliot, pp. 118–19, for example). Like any other art, poetry permits experimentation and innovation between the extremes of pure speech and pure song. Or so I have come to realize after discovering, by listening to Native American singers and storytellers, that poetry consists ultimately of the sounds of the human voice.

The Lyric Voice in Print

THE DISTINCTION I am trying to make between two kinds of poetic voice acquires added significance, I believe, as we try better to understand the relationship between performance and print, and as we learn to deal with Native American texts in that framework. If tribal peoples can be called preliterate or nonliterary, they nonetheless produce poetry worthy of recognition for its value and its appeal, at least potentially. The issue becomes one of producing adequate translation and effective transmission by way of the page. Finnegan recognizes the problem of attempting "to *read* publications of literature originally designed for oral delivery" (her emphasis). Readers can all too easily miss "the interplay of ear and eye, of audience and performer." Stripped of the dynamics of recitation, the resulting text can seem "pale and uninteresting"—fixed in a bland printed form that takes on the authority of an unchanging text (Finnegan, p. 78).

Again and again, while sitting in a Navajo hogan in the dim firelight and listening to a medicine man during a ceremony, I have found myself wondering how the visual effect of the sandpainting and the odor of burning pinyon could possibly transmit to the written page the full interplay of sight and smell in what I learned to appreciate as a poetic experience as rich and as intense as anything I had learned to expect from reading Shakespeare, Milton, Dickens, or Emily Dickinson. One such example, in particular, comes to mind. On a June evening in 1993, following a ceremonial offering from the Windway cycle, the presiding medicine man told all present how he had acquired the thick feathers in his wand from an eagle that had accidently landed in a carelessly placed ground trap. His account turned out to be nothing less than a majestic poetic narrative. Sitting cross-legged in the customary place to the west side of the sandpainting, the chanter described how he found the eagle beating its wings and furiously slashing the air with its one free claw. Addressing it by its sacred name, he said, he reasoned with it for permission to pluck its feathers in exchange for setting it free. First, however, the bird would have to subdue its anger and understand that it was to do no harm.

The singer's voice fell into a cadenced pattern as he repeated his statement to the bird. His eyes shifted gently from person to person among those present, and he worked his hands to underscore the rhythm of his speech in what I recognized as a carefully orchestrated performance. The musky aroma of burning pinyon filled the darkening hogan as dusk fell over the high bluff where it sat overlooking Shiprock, adding a lowering slant of light to the sound of his voice, the smell of the fire, the feel of the sheepskin spread beneath me where I sat, and the lingering flavor of ceremonial pollen—which all present are obliged to taste—on the tip of my tongue.

In such a setting, all the senses contribute to the total artistry of the event commensurate with anything associated with the high culture of gallery or concert hall, or in some ways more highly sensory. Furthermore, with its relationship to a tightly united cycle of narratives describing emergence and in-migration which account for the Navajo conception of earth and cosmos, the story touched upon here can take many forms depending upon the occasion and the setting. A given ceremonial gathering represents but one rendition in an ongoing dynamic process of telling and retelling, which reaffirms the notion of Bakhtin and his followers that a story actually incorporates multiple languages (see Bakhtin; see also Bruner and Gorfain). Print threatens to take the very life out of such a tradition, and I have often found myself initially frustrated with my own efforts to write down what I hear on flat sheets of paper that make no sound and bear no aroma and are far removed from the dynamics of a live performance in a language that shifts subtly from speech to chant to song as a singer recites and others alternately listen and reply.

Nonetheless, I believe that something of the deeply poetic residing in what began with the sound of a human voice can be reconstituted on the page without necessarily being eclipsed by the cool silence of print—the performance being ultimately richer than the page. There is precedence for that possibility, in fact, as Finnegan reports. In warning of what readers miss when oral literature is replicated on the silent page in an alien language, she reminds us that

> we similarly miss something by following the modern habit of reading classical Greek and Roman literature silently, through the eye only; it too was expected to be read aloud and it was a common practice in antiquity to publish a work by recitation before an audience. Furthermore, by now such classic texts have a history of being translated and retranslated, published and republished, in the context of an ever growing dialog on how they originated and were disseminated, what they meant to their contemporaries, how they were subsequently accepted and interpreted by those cultures which reissued them. In their multifarious written versions they stand like musical scores awaiting the vocal performance of anyone who cares to read them aloud or to imagine reading them aloud while doing so in silence. (p. 78)

Medieval literature was also "commonly chanted," Finnegan then adds. She might as well have reminded us that barely a century ago writers like Dickens and Longfellow composed under the assumption that a parent or grandparent would read their work aloud to others on a farmstead or in an urban family household. When committed to the voice, any text can come alive and evade the impression of final authority; and Finnegan might have added that something intrinsically poetic can indeed survive the mutation that occurs when an oral performance is put into print under certain conditions, both internal to the act of reading a text and external to it in the way audiences are conditioned to regard it.

Among the internal conditions is the obvious one of translation; it must be done sensitively and well, of course. Other internal features of the printed text are not so obvious and have come to be taken for granted. They include such less well-noticed ones as the size of print, its deployment on the page, the size and shape of the volume in which it appears. I own a ten-volume set of Friedrich Schiller's plays, poems, and essays, published in a limited deluxe edition in 1902 by the Francis A. Nicholls Company of

Boston, which I especially enjoy. It contains wide margins, ample space between stanzas, crisp lettering set in a comfortable font neither too large nor too small and on generously thick acid-free pages. Each volume includes carefully crafted and duplicated photogravure duplications of contemporary paintings. Those involved in translating and editing these volumes obviously shared a knowledge and a concern for the literary nuances of Schiller's Germany. The books are comfortable to hold and make no demands upon the eye, thereby appealing subtly to the mind's inner ear, where print is processed by way of the optimal conditions of large print and easy-to-turn pages. Volumes like that, I suspect, are typical of bookmaking at an earlier time. Compare that with today's cumbersome Norton textbook anthologies, which imply that reading "great literature" is a classroom activity demanding a willingness to curtail pleasure at the bidding of a professor. Such "texts" sometimes seem to transmute into a travesty of that term. The pages are almost too thin to clasp between the fingers for turning. With narrow margins and a font small enough to classify as subscript, the print defies easy, relaxed reading, which lends added authority to the classroom teacher familiar with the material by way of prior exposure to it under better graphic circumstances. Foregrounded silence becomes internal to what is written on the page.

Conditions external to the act of reading, meanwhile, have to do with education both formally and informally. Informal training includes basic social assumptions concerning communication and the transmission of values. Recently, those assumptions have changed considerably with the shift from print to electronic media and the dramatic rise of a consumerism that stresses more than ever individual choice in the purchase and possession of products that are ultimately the same. Where, in the past, young children may have gained consciousness as individuals and members of a group by listening to someone read or recite, today they assemble around a television set or listen to disks and tapes urging them all to wear shoes differing only in brand name or to listen to songs produced under different labels but which sound very much alike. In both cases, though, poetry plays a greater role in the socialization of individuals than teachers have managed to recognize in relegating it exclusively to print read silently either in solitude or as a classroom requirement.

Formal training includes schooling that children receive as they first learn to read and write. It also includes the critical sophistication and curiosity they may gain as their education continues. Those who acquire the greatest and deepest pleasure from reading Homer and Chaucer have generally received such training; they manage to acquire at least some knowledge of classical Greece or medieval England, along with basic critical skills.

Thanks to recent scholarship in such fields as anthropology and ethnopoetics, tribal cultures, including those of North America, no longer remain unknown or misunderstood in the way that pre-Renaissance Europeans failed to grasp the full import of their classical predecessors. Beyond that, a new multicultural awareness can arm readers with a useful relativism that invites a more open-minded investigation of those cultures, so that where it may once have seemed preposterous to assert that cultures without print could produce poetry, the possibility can now at least be entertained, together with the challenge of transmitting that poetry through conventional print or its new electronic variations. With or without the formal training potential readers may receive, I believe that something transcendentally worthwhile about *The Iliad* or *The Wife of Bath's Tale* could be rescued on the page if books could be made and distributed with a greater manifest awareness of the relationship between voice and print. Or if we are now indeed entering an electronic age where conventional editing and publishing must relent to hypermedia, interactive tv, CD-ROM or even virtual reality, maybe new ways will be found to store and disseminate the poetic voice once stored in books and regarded as a corpus of literature. And if that is possible, so it becomes possible to discover the intrinsic poetic worth of an equally vast and worthwhile corpus of North American tribal poetry. So far, however, a mere remnant survives in books and reports assembled earlier and often dismissed as mere data. Little by little, it is gaining added notice with more recent efforts to recognize its literary worth. But its full magnitude as effective and noteworthy poetry remains to be discovered, just as it remains to recover the poetic voice from the dead silence of the mass-produced page.

Ideally, bringing a lyrical work to the page should be an especially deliberate process, not only for the redactor but for the
reader, who must remain aware that what has been placed there
originates in an oral setting where the tightly structured sound of
a human voice was central. For one thing, the recorder can use
conventional print graphics in the way that Washington Matthews deployed them with his translations of Navajo lyrics. In the
following passage, for example, as he does elsewhere, he displays a
chant on the page in distinct linear units that virtually render parallel syntax visible and might easily be produced in print as verse
stanzas. I have converted his improvised phonemic transcription
to what is now official Navajo orthography.

Hayoolkááł beehoghán.	House made of dawn.
Nahootsooí beehoghán.	House made of evening light.
Kosailhil beehoghán.	House made of the dark cloud.
Niltsábiká beehoghán.	House made of male rain.
Áhidilyil beehoghán.	House made of dark fog.
Niltsiba'ad beehoghán.	House made of female rain.

In addition to the conventionally scored musical notation used in
her anthology of Native American lyrical and colloquial poetry,
Natalie Curtis (1907) also employed the established practice of ar-
ranging distinct units of syntax stanzaically. This bilingual transcription of a Papago song serves as a characteristic example of
how she adapted oral material to the printed page:

Sikya volimu	Yellow butterflies,
Humisi manatu	Over the blossoming virgin corn,
Talasi yammu	With pollen-painted faces
Pitzangwa timakiang	Chase one another in brilliant throng.
Shakwa volimu	Blue butterflies
Mozhisi manatu	Over the blossoming virgin beans,
Talasi yammu	With pollen-painted faces
Pitzangwa timakiang	Chase one another in brilliant streams. (p. 484)

In his fine translations of Tewa poetry, Herbert Spinden (1933) did likewise, as the following example shows, especially in the way that separate stanzas describe how each of the four cardinal directions commands a separate stanzaic unit, together comprising a schematic, print-driven vision of how the far-flung cosmic forces converge in germinating corn:

> There towards the north
> There the fog is lying,
> There the fog is lying.
> In the middle stands Blue Corn
> Happily, prettily, she is singing.
> Ha-we-ra-na na-a-se
>
> There towards the west
> There the fog is lying,
> There the fog is lying,
> In the middle stands Yellow Corn
> Happily, prettily, she is singing.
> Ha-wa-ra-na na-a-se
>
> There towards the south
> There the fog is lying,
> There the fog is lying,
> In the middle stands Red Corn
> Happily, prettily, she is singing
> Ha-we-ra-na sa-a-se
>
> There towards the east
> There the fog is lying,
> There the fog is lying,
> In the middle stands White Corn
> Happily, prettily, she is singing
> Ha-wa-ra-na na-a-se (pp. 78–79)

Earlier efforts to relocate lyrical material on the page could result in misleading "literary" translations like Henry Rowe Schoolcraft's notorious rendition of a song he overheard some

Ojibwe children singing while at play (1853, p. 230; reproduced in Greenway, pp. 13–14):

> Fire-fly, fire-fly! bright little thing.
> Light me to bed, and my song I will sing.
> Give me your light, as you fly o'er my head,
> That I may merrily go to my bed.

To his credit, Schoolcraft included a transcription of the original along with a literal English rendering, which suggests that he sensed the distorting effect of translation. But the fact remains that what he considered a literary version reflects contemporary taste at its hackneyed worst, where intrusively imposed patterns of rhyme and meter alone are mistaken for poetry. Unfortunately, that version would later circulate in anthologies like George Cronyn's *Path of the Rainbow* (1934, p. 12) without Schoolcraft's accompanying transcription and literal account and without his rejoinder that it originated as an improvisation by children at play. Under the assumption, then, that a Chippewa lyric must be bent to fit the conventions of printed English verse with no regard for how it originally sounds, the impression lingers that like Schoolcraft's "Chant to the Fire-Fly," Native American poetry has the depth and range of jump-rope lyrics or nursery rhymes at their most simplistic.[3]

In what I consider a landmark essay on the subject, Dell Hymes (1981, pp. 35–64) constructs an alternative procedure for representing the lyrical voice in printed English. Foremost, he says, the task requires knowing the donor language or, at the very least, having access to a careful linguistic analysis of it. It also demands an attentiveness to a work's structure, which includes "the form of repetition and variation, of constants and contrasts, in verbal organization" (p. 42). And it calls for a conscious awareness of the medium of print, with its practice of aligning phrases linearly, its stanzaic blocks, and even its peculiar way of utilizing such graphic features as italics to signify vocal emphasis.

For example, he cites an old Boasian Kwakiutl cradle song (pp. 49–50) to illustrate the incremental repetition common to Native

American lyric poetry but seldom present in English or European alphabetical poetry.[4] The transliteration looks like this.

1. hants'e:noqwi'lakwe:ky la:qEn gya:q'e:na'ye:
   bEgwa:nEmts'e:da dask'wa, *ya ha ha ha.*
2. a:le:winuqwi' lakwe:ky la:qEn gya:q'e''ma'ye:
   bEgwa:nEmts'e:da dask'wa, *ya ha ha ha.*
3. le:q'e:noqwi' lakwe:ky la:qEn gya:q'e:na'ye:
   bEgwa:nEmtsqe:da dask'wa, *ya ha ha ha.*
4. Lats'ae:noqwi'lakwe:ky la:qEn gya:q'e:na'ye:
   bEgwa:nEmts'e:da dask'wa, *ya ha ha ha.*
5. e:aqElae:noqwi'tLEky la:qEn gya:q'e: na'ye:
   bEgwa:nEmts'e:da dask'wa, *ya ha ha ha.*
6. qats ky'eatse:tso:s tsa:yakwe:yatso:s yaqe:s
   'na:kwatsao:s aqe:qs dEso:tso:s dask'wa, *ya ha ha ha.*

Boas, meanwhile, provided this literal translation:

1. Born-to-be-a-hunter at-my becoming a-man, Father,
   ya ha ha ha.
2. Born-to-be-a-spearsman at-my becoming a-man, Father,
   ya ha ha ha.
3. Born-to-be-a-canoe-builder at-my becoming a-man, Father,
   ya ha ha ha.
4. Born-to-be-a-board splitter at-my becoming a-man,
   Father, *ya ha ha* ha.
5. Born-to-be-a-worker at-my becoming a-man, Father,
   ya ha ha ha.
6. That-you-will-nothing need of all you wanted-by-you,
   by-you, Father, *ya ha ha ha.*

And he offers this literary translation:

"When I am a man, I shall be a hunter, O father!
   ya ha ha ha!"
"When I am a man, I shall be a harpooner, O father!
   ya ha ha ha!"

"When I am a man, I shall be a canoe-builder, O father!
  ya ha ha ha!"
"When I am a man, I shall be a board-maker, O father!
  ya ha ha ha!"
"That there may be nothing of which you will be in want,
  O father! *ya ha ha ha!*"

Hymes calls this the most suitable literary translation, however:

"Born to be a hunter,
    when I become a man,
      Father,
        Ya ha ha ha.

Born to be a harpooner,
    when I become a man,
      Father,
        Ya ha ha ha.

Born to be a boatwright,
    when I become a man,
      Father,
        Ya ha ha ha.

Born to be a board-splitter,
    when I become a man,
      Father,
        Ya ha ha ha.

To be a craftsman,
    when I become a man,
      Father,
        Ya ha ha ha.

That you, you will need nothing,
    of all you want,
      Father,
        Ya ha ha ha."

Hymes justifies the change by asserting that each unit originally represented as a line in Boas actually contains four distinct phrasal segments that can be combined to form separate stanzas. Presumably, each segment is marked by boundaries of pause or a duplicated shift in tone or pitch, or some such similar combination of suprasegmental properties. Additionally, each four-part unit throughout the first five of those segments consists of one variable and three invariables, while the sixth contains only two invariables (p. 51), offsetting itself the way, say, a half note is offset when it follows a succession of quarter notes in a series of musical bars that are otherwise identical.

Again, we would hardly expect to find such a technique of vocables and rigidly parallel syntax in our vaunted Anglo-European literary canon, or even in much of what the proponents of a newer multicultural canon would recognize. The language in this orally composed cradle song is very much unlike that of the alphabetically assembled lyrical poetry of such mainstream British poets as Milton, Shakespeare, Wordsworth, and Tennyson. Nor does it dovetail with the literary work of contemporary writers like Toni Morrison or Maxine Hong Kingston, who represent the newly acknowledged minorities in today's multicultural community which allegedly drew heavily from their own orality. It may overlap somewhat with pages in Leslie Silko's work or that of N. Scott Momaday, but such contemporary Native American writers remain essentially alphabetical poets. Furthermore, the phrasing of such a work is all too easy to dismiss as simpleminded repetition devoid of complexity or significance. But this kind of incremental repetition—deceptively simple because of its terseness—projects far more thought and design than our own alphabetical poetry conditions us to expect, including, in some instances, nothing less than a carefully articulated cosmic vision.

Acknowledging the subtlety of incremental repetition and its ultimate worth as a viable poetic device depends upon the kind of familiarity that the classical scholar can bring to the task of translating Sappho or Catullus effectively, however. The Kwakiutl cradle song harvested by Boas and reworked by Hymes balances maritime activities against land-based ones, and the hunting of natural game with man-made objects. It telescopes, so to speak, the differences between the ready-made and the fabricated, the progress of the new-born son from infant to man, and the transition of the father from new parent to dependent elder, summarizing life's passages as cycles of youth and age on land and sea in a world composed of providers and the provided-for. It reflects a world view and system of values different from those of literary Europe. Recognizing all of that results from an open-minded investigation not only of the verbal artifact itself, both as something recited and something ultimately translated and transcribed, but of the work's full cultural setting, which, however different from the cultures of early Greece or Rome, is in many ways as complex and as rich.

In the Kwakiutl cradle song the incremental repetition occurs in simple, straightforwardly parallel units that may highlight an apparent simplicity at the expense of concealing an accompanying complexity. But it can also occur in patterns that make a greater intricacy more mainfest, too, especially in longer works that are probably less tightly lyrical. As reconstituted literarily by John Bierhorst from an earlier text assembled by Horatio Hale, for example, the Iroquois *Ritual of Condolence* contains what I call a root sentence that repeats a theme with slight variations throughout the fifteen articles of the entire work, which occupies forty-seven pages all told when cast in print. "It is that in the midst of great darkness thou art sitting too prone in grief, thy back alone visible in the thick darkness," the condoling persona cries out allegorically to a grieving brother in a ritual drama wherein one moiety of the entire confederacy addresses the other, which has lost a council member through death. Thereupon the older brother bids, "do . . . wipe away thy tears" so that the grieving one "wilt again behold what is taking place on earth" (Bierhorst: 1974, pp. 130–31).

In contrast with the rigid structure of the short Kwakiutl lyric, however, the lengthier and apparently more loosely structured dramatic Iroquois work is unified not by tightly incremental phrases occuring in line after line, but by one slightly varied root phrase or sentence repeated from stanza to stanza throughout then recurs in some varied form in subsequent stanzas. "It inevitably comes to pass that the sky is lost to the senses of [the bereaved] person," asserts the root sentence of article seven of the Iroquois condolence. "Now, therefore, the sky is completely lost to thy view," the next stanza echoes. And in the very next stanza, the condoling brother assures him, "Now, then, we beautify again the sky for you" in a structurally reminiscent phrase (Bierhorst: 1974, pp. 150–51). Such patterns of repetition and near-repetition are similarly scattered throughout the neighboring articles. However, they are easily overlooked because the reiterated sentences occur in paragraph-like stanzas that more closely resemble colloquial prose than a lyrically inclined form of incremental repetition—at least to the unpracticed reader.

Meanwhile, the overall work progresses from article to article: first, the grieving brother's sight is restored as the condoling brother removes his tears; his hearing is regained in the next article as the latter removes "the obstacles obstructing the passages of thy ears" (Bierhorst: 1974, p. 133); his throat is reopened so that he can speak; his breast is cleared so that he can breathe and can experience emotions once more; and so on through the remainder of the drama, until he can function once again to make the confederacy as whole and as operative as a physically and spiritually healthy human being—reinforced throughout by a series of root sentences that produce the kind of thematic rhythm I spoke of earlier. Just as a conceptualized cosmic pattern emerges through the tightly structured incremental passages of the cradle song, so does an intricate pattern develop wherein the constituent tribal polity takes its place in the broader scheme of earth and sky envisioned through the Iroquois story of creation and the Thank-You Prayer.

With careful reading and an alertness to the difference between performance and print, even the most seemingly unpoetic written renditions of such a work as the *Ritual of Condolence* can exhibit repetition along with other patterns of syntax and theme. Assiduous translation helps, too, of course, especially when accompanied by that same self-conscious awareness of how writing and speaking or singing interrelate. With such care on the part of reader and writer, it is possible to recognize other properties of lyric poetry in a written translation, too, not easily detected in the European manuscript convention of employing fixed patterns of meter and rhyme in composing and understanding print-driven lyric poetry such as that found in standard textbook anthologies. One such important property is the patterned configuration of sound and silence that can be heard in a good poetic performance and can be duplicated in transcription and translation somewhat effectively by the deployment of positive and negative space on individual lines, or, in other words, bytes which contain alphabetical characters and those which are left blank.

Look again at the apparently simple passage, quoted above (p. 52), translated by Washington Matthews. It actually belongs to a much larger text which, in turn, connects with a vast Navajo network of chantway narratives that find ultimate expression in the elaborate healing ceremonies related to creation mythology (see Wyman and Kluckhohn). To simplify somewhat, each chant reenacts an ancient story of how a stricken individual courts destruction by transgressing against an immediate family, a clan, or any of the world's numerous spirit-beings. Consciously or inadvertently, that individual has done something to upset the fragile, greater-than-human balance that exists at all levels, ranging from that of the immediate social group to the vast cosmic array. Whether cast out, abandoned, or in fearful self-willed flight, the hero or heroine undergoes a series of scathing, near-fatal adventures before being rescued far from home by the *Haaschch'ééh dine'é* or Holy People—primary deities associated with such forces as the winds, the changing seasons, different kinds of rain, or the sun and moon and stars in their various constellations (see Spencer).

The patient must now summon these supernaturals to repeat the healing process originally described in the parent narrative, and does so either vicariously when a medicine man sings out an appeal to them to approach, or actually sings out when he or she is under a shaman's supervision. The six lines quoted here comprise part of one such invocation, as it were, to the dwelling place of these deities, *Tséyi'* or Canyon de Chelly, which is a microcosm of the balanced components of dawn and evening light, dark cloud and dark mist, male and female rain, and pollen and grasshoppers

—sets of counterpoised opposites tightly configured in a scheme of distinct utterances that match likenesses and differences and that readily can be transformed into distinct linear units in printed English. Thus, the empty space in each printed line takes the place of the observable interval of silence separating one unit from the next. In an actual performance, the recognizable pauses add significantly to the impact of the poem; in fact, you don't necessarily have to understand what the words mean to register the cadenced alternation between voice and silence, any more than a listener needs to assign referential meaning to vocables in a song to recognize a melody or grasp its meter. Seen or heard that way, each line becomes all the more manifest as a carefully measured, self-contained linguistic entity phonemically, morphemically, syntactically, and referentially.

Attentively read with the knowledge that it did not originate on the printed page, such seemingly simple, repetitive poetry as that which Matthews presents here manages to represent a scheme of dynamic balance observed in the physical world. The Navajos have no single-word counterpart to our term *nature*, as their lexicon confirms. Instead, they rely on a large vocabulary that recognizes an active cosmos consisting of twelve venues including four subterranean zones below the earth, four surrounding bodies of water, and four vaults of sky overhead. Throughout that cosmic system, forces play against each other in an ongoing struggle for balance (see Franciscan Fathers, pp. 35–37). Seasons come and go in endless cycles measured by the complementary movement of sun and moon and stars. Life alternates with death in parallel cycles of germination and decay, while darkness and light contend analogously with an ongoing effort of male and female to surmount differences and function together in harmony. Grasshoppers invade blossoms to stir and transmit pollen. Alternately, clouds gather to issue rain and mist rises from the earth to refurbish them. Taken together, this ongoing drama of force and counterforce can be seen as an ostensibly organic "greater than human reality" whose components collectively equate with our isolated term *nature*.

Once a Euroamerican reader conditioned to standard Western notions recognizes that the singular English word *nature* has no lexical counterpart in Navajo, an interesting opening for poetic discovery results. Instead of being signified by a single term, the idea of nature in Navajo summons a vast network of terms that combine to designate a complementary series of paired elemental forces: day and night, dawn and dusk, male and female, earth and sky, and so forth. When expressed poetically those forces invite the use of terse segmented units of expression that can be highlighted on the page through the exacting interplay of printed characters and unused space, line by line. Prayers and chants thereby align those matched forces; to recognize as much helps to shape an understanding of how that culture's lyric poetry might be written down in the conversion from performance to print. Hence the Navajo *Night Chant* prayer (cited on p. 52, above), which Washington Matthews so aptly translates, concludes this way:

> May it be beautiful before me.
> May it be beautiful behind me.
> May it be beautiful below me.
> May it be beautiful above me.

Coupled with the opposition of beauty arrayed before and behind or above and below is the amount of empty or negative space on each line offset by the nearly equal degree of printed or positive space—a subtly effective way of reinforcing graphically what Navajo lyric poetry asserts vocally.

Such paired elemental forces, which comprise nature's vast constituent array, can also prompt inquiry into the relationship between narratives that tell of the overall creation and lyrics that celebrate one or another of its particular results or consequences, very much as the Seneca Thank-You Prayer celebrates the story of how the universe was created long ago in some ancient primordial time. The eight-line invocation in Matthews's translation of the fourth-day prayer of the Night Chant identifies one such force in each line, for example, and then matches it with another in a successive line, invoking a shared understanding of how each part fits into a larger dynamic unity, thanks to the delicate way that sound balances against silence in the application of voice.

The house is made of dawn, goes the first line (*Hayoolkááł beehoghán*), and of evening light per the second (*Nahootsoi beehoghán*), balancing two referentially oppositional elements seen to cycle back and forth in dynamic union. As the third and fourth line of the passage specify, *Tséiyi'* is also made respectively of dark cloud (*L'osalihil beehoghán*) and male rain (*Niltsábiká beehogán*), uniting two more of nature's components combined in a basic cause-and-effect relationship. The next two lines link the gentler, less formidable components of dark mist and female rain, which offsets the more severe dark-cloud, male-rain pairing. Then the final two lines match the active pollen-spreading grasshopper with the passively spread pollen, and together they in turn trigger the reproduction induced by the light of the sun which recurs daily and intensifies once spring equinox occurs, and by the male and female rain. Thus tightly measured linguistic segments adapted by the lyric voice express a deep awareness of a greater-than-human reality created in a primordial long ago, which buttresses human consciousness in the immediacy of here and now.

Fluent in the language and familiar with the culture, Matthews sets an example for translators who wish to reproduce in printed English what they hear recited in a donor language. Sensitive to the nuances of a time-honored Navajo story and chantway tradition and its application to ceremonial practice, he recognized how those segments merged as coalescing lexical, syntactic, and referential units in Navajo song and prayer; and he could detail that knowledge through translation as well as through the graphics of print. The result is an English text that bears maximum fidelity to the original poem, given the differences that separate the two linguistically. Hymes, too, could secure such principles in transforming a performance of the Kwakiutl cradle song into a viable alphabetical English lyric poem. A number of other scholar-translators (or anthropological philologists, as Hymes calls them) are also experimenting with such principles, securing step-by-step procedures for replicating in written English the formidable body of Native lyrical poetry that ultimately rests as part of North America's still unrecognized classical poetic tradition, offering a wealth of sacred texts (see Toelken and Scott; Swann: 1985; see too the various essays in Swann: 1992; and see the more recently gathered texts in Krupat: 1993, pp. 3–205).

The Colloquial Voice and the Printed Page

IF LYRIC POETRY at its purest is the poetry of the singing voice consisting of measured segments of speech sounds, controlled syntax, and rigidly balanced lexical units, then colloquial poetry at its most flatly conversational is the language of the speaking voice containing fewer manifestly artificial features, often with a different sort of content. It goes beyond the structural constraints of measured lyric; it follows the loose, more natural cadences of speech; and it exists without the accompaniment of dance or instrumentation. In colloquial poetry, the voice heard is that of a storyteller relating an action or a sequence of events occurring sometime in the past; that of an orator speaking discursively to transmit a body of information or to impart ideas; or that of a character in a dialogue or a dramatic exchange. In alphabetical traditions, like those of America and of Europe, such colloquial works would likely be classed as short stories and novels or as essays, and their unmeasured style would qualify as prose.

When arranged on the printed page, colloquial poetry at its purest might fill each line from the left margin to the right, with no need for the kind of spacing that delineates measured linear or stanzaic units for the reading eye. Content becomes more open, as does style, allowing for such things as a greater range of thought, the added possibility for a more individualized play of ideas or an idiosyncratic style imposed upon a conventionally known story— what Bakhtin calls "semantic open-mindedness" (p. 7), although I am reluctant to invoke a currently cited European critic. I suspect that Black Elk spoke colloquially to John Neihardt, as Avery Jimerson spoke to me while telling about the Seneca dislocation to make room for the Kinzua Dam. My impression is that many of the Native American stories compiled and collected earlier in this century were recited colloquially, such as those assembled by Arthur C. Parker in *Seneca Myths and Folk Tales*.

Julian Rice, who has done monumental work in assembling and

interpreting Lakota narratives, uses the term *colloquial* with reference to Ella Deloria's technique of listening to her elders tell traditional stories without transcribing or recording "the original narrations." Instead, he adds, she "rewrote the stories in Lakota as she remembered them," and "in doing so participated directly in the storytelling tradition rather than simply transferring it to written form." In adapting the technique "of the traditional narrator and perhaps of oral traditions in general," Rice adds, Deloria retains "certain set speeches and formulaic word patterns" which "remain fixed in her memory while the rest of the telling was improvised in her own words" (Rice, pp. 184–85).

English versions of material such as Parker's translations of Seneca stories, Neihardt's retelling of Black Elk's story, or Ella Deloria's Lakota narratives are not likely to be considered poetic by ordinary readers. For print technology has generated the arbitrary and fairly superficial distinction between "poetry" and "prose," where the former term confounds written verse with what I more broadly call poetry to the exclusion of what the latter now conventionally designates. The densely blocked paragraphs that Parker employs—or whose individual lines are dispersed margin to margin on the page as prose in publications like *Navaho Legends*—can tend to mute the artistry present in colloquial poetry, especially when the print is as small and tightly placed on the page as it is in the Matthews publication. As Ivan Brady says (1991, p. 306), readers "forget too easily that the eye's feast on the written word is at one level or another likely to be a rendering of what the ear hears." That print-oriented oversight helps to explain errors such as the one found in the entry on "American Indian Poetry" in the *Princeton Encyclopedia of Poetry and Poetics*. There, the writer identifies "a surprising lack . . . in narrative verse" among the tribes. "The Indian customarily told his tales and legends in prose," he writes, as if the Native American voice were incapable of doing otherwise, "and reserved the poetic style and rhythm for nonprosaic purposes" (Preminger et al., p. 20). It simply never occurs to him that he has only read prose translations of those "tales and legends" (a set of implicitly pejorative terms, incidentally, especially as they appear to apply here) without ever hearing any of them in their native performative setting.

Judgments like that arise from views of "poetic style and rhythm" confined to printed lyric; but even an experienced listener like Washington Matthews can confuse the looser *poesis* of the colloquial voice with printed prose. In his nonetheless excellent introduction to *Navaho Legends*, as well as in other things he has written on the Navajos, or in his sensitively arranged translations of Navajo lyric poetry, Matthews certainly recognizes Navajo poetic power. But in his effort to reproduce colloquial narrative in prose form, he overlooked the more subtly dispersed artistry in colloquial poetry, just as we are apt to do today since, like him, we are trained as readers of poetry rather than as listeners to it. For example, instead of including repetitions in his prose translations, Matthews would merely indicate parenthetically that a request, a reply, an admonition or a particular action occurred three or four more times, and then continue to fill each line clear to the end of a paragraph. Similarly, in Father Berard Haile's translations of Navajo stories (see Wyman: 1970, for example, or consider the different versions of *The Deerway* he gathered and which Luckert assembled in *The Navajo Hunter Tradition*), or in Frank Cushing's and Matilda Coxe Stevenson's translations of Zuni narratives, printed prose overwhelms what Brady calls "the musicality of verse" (p. 305)—the dynamics of speech and the more loosely structured patterns of thought and action that give the colloquial voice its poetic richness (see Tedlock: 1971, 1991; see also Huntsman). Readers need to watch prose translations carefully for those patterns, which resonate with an inward rhythm more of content than of outward sound.

"The Seven Star Dancers," for example, from Parker's collection of Seneca stories, tells of a youth who falls in love with one of "seven shining young women dancing" on a river's surface. Even in a so-called prose translation that contains none of the outward poetic trappings of measured verse, the details occur in a rhythm-like progression. First, the young man sees the "seven shining young women dancing in the water" although they make "no spashing" sound. Then he hears them speak "but [can]not understand what they [say]." Rushing from his hiding place, he tries to catch the youngest, who appeals to him as the most beautiful, but she along with the others jumps into a giant corn basket and returns in it to the sky. The next night they return, and he both sees and hears them immediately this time. He then lunges for her again and this time manages to seize her so that she cannot get away, whereupon he declares his love and she agrees that they will be married (Parker: 1923, pp. 86–87). In recounting the sequence of those two successive encounters, the story progresses from sight only to sight and sound without touch or verbal exchange on the first night to sight and sound together on the second, followed by touch along with conversation. Thus, a careful reading discloses a progressively patterned subtext in what I consider an underlying themelike rhythm analogous to any more overtly repeated pattern of syntax or sound. Is it altogether accurate to dismiss such a rendering as ordinary prose?

I did not sense the thematic rhythm prominent in Navajo storytelling tradition when I first read Washington Matthews's translations of key narratives in *Navaho Legends*—or in what Zumthor may mean when he speaks of "the repetitiveness of a deep-seated collection experience, whence . . . a particular redundancy and less thematic variations" (p. 33). I had to become an experienced listener with a working sense of the Navajo language before I could notice the sustained rhythm of colloquial discourse in a storyteller's voice and observe how it combined with body language along with thematic rhythm to add a dimension that no ordinary or heedless prose translation could indicate (see Zolbrod: 1992b).

I now wonder if narratives gathered earlier like Matthews's or Parker's were as flatly prosaic in the way they were originally recited as they seem to be in printed English. In a vivid prefatory chapter, "The Atmosphere in which the Legends Were Told," Parker describes the conditions of an actual performance on a winter evening in the communal longhouse. Hearing the storyteller arrive, the children would run to the door and lead him inside. "Hoskwisaonh," they would shout; "the storyteller,—the storyteller has come!" Adults would join in welcoming him, one woman directing him to a bench before the central fire while several others placed cornhusks around it. Specially dressed for the occasion, he also carried a parcel of small props such as bear teeth and shells. Once seated, he would take out a pipe and some sacred tobacco, light it, and then blow a puff of smoke and open his story with a "ritualistic prayer to the unseen powers, about whom he is soon to discourse." And finally he would exclaim, "Hauh, oneh djadaondyus," to which everybody present would reply, "Hauh oneh!" Only then could the story begin (Parker: 1923, pp. 49–50). We would do well to suspect that such a special event would evoke a certain stylized, foregrounded discourse. I have had the pleasure of hearing Navajo storyteller Sunni Dooley recite under formal circumstances. Currently studying with a number of Navajo medicine men, I first heard her in the spring of 1990, when she agreed to tell a traditional story for the closing banquet at the sixth annual Navajo Studies Conference at Window Rock, Arizona. For the occasion she wore an elaborately patterned full-length skirt; an ornate, formally decorated long-sleeved blouse; and a hand-woven shawl replete with symbolic figures. She stood behind a podium for this occasion, probably since there were so many people in attendance. Summoning a fluid body motion, she recited alternately in English and Navajo with commanding poise. Her movement enhanced a manifest cadence of sound and syntax that lacked the precise metrical structure of a fixed verse form, but certainly highlighted patterns of voice that are all too easily lost in the silence of written prose. This was obviously a practiced performance; as did others, I felt myself in the presence of an artist of the magnitude of a recognized singer or a virtuoso cellist or violinist. The next day she gave another formal presentation at the public library in Window Rock, where she simply stood before her audience with no podium separating them. But she wore the same elaborate costume, and for that session brought an ornate cradle board with her as a prop and gave the same commanding performance before an audience which recognized it as such. Since then I have heard her recite elsewhere, and I have experienced the anticipation she instills among those who know her work. For those familiar with them, her performances become an occasion whose anticipation generates an aura to which she responds palpably.

It is misleading to think of such a recitation in terms of ordinary speech or to reduce its transcription to ordinary expository discourse, just as it would be simplistic to call the longhouse storyteller's language mere prose, and as it is an oversight to miss the poetic properties of good storytelling in any language. A viable recitation elevates language even when its rhythms and tropes make it more conversational than lyric poetry sounds. That is certainly true of storytellers to whom I have listened, whether Seneca, Apache, or Navajo. I consider them poets: they speak in a voice clearly nonlyrical but distinctly nonconversational as well. Even when nonmetrical, their language displays what I now refer to as thematic rhythm manifesting something deeply poetic and less superficially manifest than metered verse displays on the page. Therein, conceptual patterns recur along with patterns of speech broader than the tight measures common to the lyrical voice (see also Tedlock's term, "a rhyme of meanings": 1991, p. 316).

Dennis Tedlock noticed such patterns in the Zuni stories that Andrew Paynetsa recited, however, and highlighted them on the page by orchestrating syntax with his specially modified print graphics. In his translation of "The Boy and the Deer," for example, a mother is impregnated "without knowing any man," furtively gives birth nearby a juniper tree, digs a hole, and "[abandons] the baby there" (pp. 4, 19, 26). In formula-like quasi-repetition throughout the remainder of the story, that event is then reiterated in lines of fixed but varying length to indicate pauses or shifts in pitch. First, the narrator repeats in his own voice that the mother "had pains, got out of the water / went to a TREE and there . . . just DROPPED" her infant son (p. 16). Then he assumes the voice of the child's adoptive deer-mother as she instructs him to remind his natural mother, "you went to a tree and just dropped me there" (p. 19). Then he repeats what the son actually says as he tells the mother, "When you dropped me / you made a little hole and placed me there" (p. 26)—repeating the key verb each time, but changing its position in the phrase which contains it and signalling changes in loudness and pitch.

Likewise, the female deer rescues the infant, nurses him as her own, and resolves to "go to Kachina Village, for he is without *clothing, naked*" (p. 7) to tell the gods, "I've come to ask for *clothes* for him," and then "*clothe[s]* him" (p. 8), giving his deer identity an obvious thematic dimension, as I emphasize by adding italics to a key term. That theme is subsequently reiterated with the repetition that the boy "was dressed in white and he wore a macaw headdress" (p. 13); then when the deer mother later reminds him, "I went to Kachina Village to get *clothes* for you" (p. 17); next as she instructs him that upon encountering his mother he must say to her, "I had no *clothing* / so my [deer] mother went to Kachina Village to ask for *clothing*" (p. 19), and finally when he tells his human mother, "My mother here went to Kachina Village to ask for my *clothing*. . . . That's why I'm *clothed*" (p. 27; italics added).

A corresponding example of thematic rhythm or "a rhythm of meanings" exists in the first part of Tedlock's two-part transla-tion of the Zuni creation story (pp. 223–98). There, the Ahayuuta or warrior twins are sent into the earth by their father the Sun to bring forth people who will properly worship him. Accordingly, they instruct each of five different groups of primal, shapeless be-ings to make their way to the earth's surface and become fully formed humans. To the first they state their purpose simply and straightforwardly: "we must take you with us out into the day-light," they say; "BECAUSE OF THESE WORDS, because of these instructions, we have entered upon your ROADS" (p. 235). With each successive explanation they elaborate a little until they at last declare,

> ". . . and so [our Sun Father] sent us in.
> When we came to the village they did not know
> how to get out.
> A————ll your elder bro
> > thers
> from all around
> have been brought together
> but because they did not know
> your elder brother, the Coral Priest
> NEXT SPOKE OF YOU, and so
> I have come
> to summon you," . . . (p. 246)

By carefully coordinating print with what he observed as he lis-tened, Tedlock managed to capture the subtle but persistent *poesis* of Zuni colloquial storytelling in his English translations. That quality does not stand out the way such manifest patterns as rhyme and meter do in English lyrical poetry, of course. But it is certainly there. In "The Speaker of Tales," where he analyzes a story he transcribed earlier, Tedlock argues that unlike English and American lyric, which scans according to rhyme schemes and poetic feet, Zuni colloquial poetry "scans parallelistically," getting its rhythm from reiterated thematic units or recursive units of slightly varying syntax, not from tightly woven measures of meter and end sounds (see Tedlock: 1991, especially p. 317).

Bear in mind, too, that colloquial poetry sounds more poetic when read aloud than when it is monitored visually in silent solitude on the printed page, where it can be virtually buried in the compactness of conventionally arranged prose. Thoughtfully used print graphics can remind a reader that poetry originates with the human voice, however, especially if arranged to reaffirm such vocal features as stress, pitch, and pause along with recurring syntactic units (see, for example, Krupat: 1992). And the thoughtful solitary reader can always seek thematic unity in whatever way seems possible. Better still, such a reader can work to develop a technique for doing so; and by sharing that technique with others willing to help refine it, such a reader participates in the work of the literary—or better even yet from my own perspective, the poetic—critic. Paralleling the lead of innovative translators like Dennis Tedlock and Dell Hymes, various other print-conscious scholars have managed to demonstrate that principle, such as Barre Toelken and Tacheeni Scott, in their careful retranslation of Yellowman's version of a Navajo trickster story (1981); Elaine Jahner, in the way she transcribes Lakota Stone Boy narratives (1983); or Donald Bahr, in his edition of *Rainhouse and Ocean: Speeches for the Papago Year*—Ruth Underhill's still-unheralded translations of Papago calendrical orations (1979).

In fact, the remarkable Underhill collection displays especially well how the poetic voice can range along a continuum from tightly structured lyric, at one extreme, to the loosely colloquial, at the other, within a single ceremonial framework, and how something of that shifting voice can be recovered in English. On the lyric side, we find passages like this one from the incrementally repetitive speech to initiate the deer hunt:

Towards the sunset [I] made a road and placed the
    black eagle, beyond that placed my shining helper [coyote]
Towards the sea [south] made a road, placed the
    black eagle, beyond that placed my shining helper
Towards the morning [east] made a road, placed the
    black eagle, beyond that placed my shining helper
Towards the north made a road, placed the black eagle,
    beyond that placed my shining helper.

Im hudunig wui wo:gk na:to kc wua g s-cuk ba'ag,
    am oidk ke:swa g s-tonlig n-we:mgal
Im ka:cim wui wo:gk na:to, ke:swa g s-cuk ba'ag,
    a, odik ke:swa g s-tonlig n-we:mgal
Im si'alig wui wo:gk na:to, ke:swa g s-cuk ba'ag,
    am oidk ke:swa g s-tonlig n-we:mgal
Im winim wui wo:gk na:to, ke:swa g s-cuk ba'ag,
    s-tonlig n-we:mgal. (pp. 78–79)

On the other hand, Papago calendrical oratory can also be
delivered more conversationally, with repetitive phrases widely
enough scattered to be barely noticed. In the more colloquial running speech, for example, recited to begin the Papago year, the
orator employs few of the measured or tightly repetitive elements
associated with lyric, save for occasional echo-phrases in the telling of a shamanic venture into the sky to coax rain out of the
cloud spirits. These are, so to speak, aural mirror images wherein
a phrase used in one part of a speech is repeated in another except
for a mutual exchange of two or so lexical units complementarily.
"The someplace sitting people that desire like *me I* then remembered," the speaker might say in describing the outward journey
with much the same freedom to improvise that a jazz musician
has; "The road *towards you* shined brightly and was put" [Hebai
da:kam *n-wepo* taccuikam am haha wa i cegito / *Ta i m*-wui wo:g
si tonodk e-ce:k] (p. 25; italics added). Then, in later describing his
return journey where he brings the life-giving rain with him, he
states in a corresponding passage, "The someplace sitting people
that desire like *you you* then remembered / The road *to me*

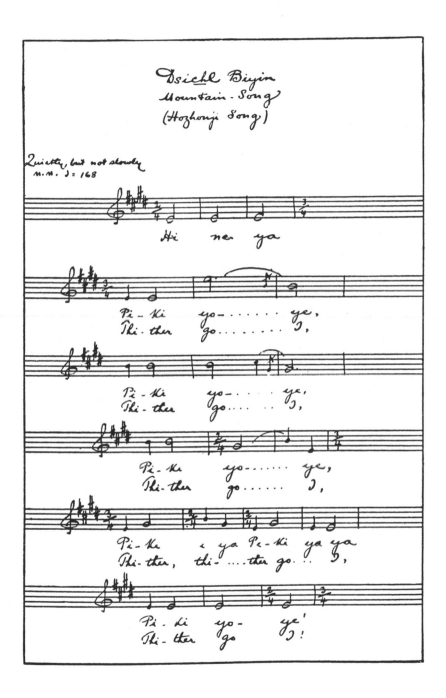

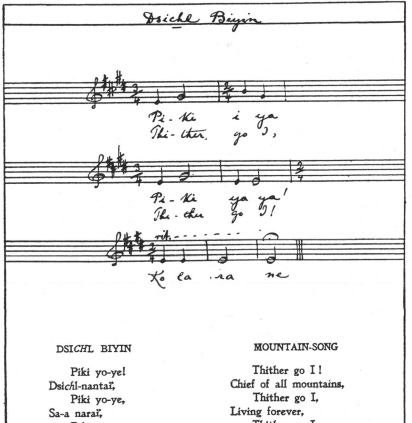

Dsichl Biyin

Pi - Ki   i   ya
Thi - ther.   go   I,

Pi - Ki   ya   ya'
Thi - ther   go   I!

rit.
Ko   la   ra   ne

DSI*CHL* BIYIN

Piki yo-ye!
Dsi*ch*l-nantaï,
   Piki yo-ye,
Sa-a naraï,
   Piki yo-ye,
Bike hozhoni,
   Piki yo-ye,
Tsoya shi*ch* ni-la !
   Piki yo-ye !

MOUNTAIN-SONG

Thither go I !
Chief of all mountains,
   Thither go I,
Living forever,
   Thither go I,
Blessings bestowing.
   Thither go I,
Calling me " Son, my son."
   Thither go I !

shined bright and was put / Reaching me here" [*Kupt a* hebai *g e-wepo* taccuikam haha wa i cegito / *Kut a n*-wui wo:g si tonodk e-ce:k / K ia n-ai] (p. 27).

Once voice is recognized as a matter of degree, ranging from the purely lyrical to purely colloquial, *Rainhouse and Ocean* becomes a case in point that typography should be adjusted carefully in the conversion to print. Where oratory is recited fully as song, the text might ideally include some kind of score, which is what Natalie Curtis's *The Indians' Book* does.[5] Or else some other graphic technique might be used to display the characteristics of language sung or chanted rather than spoken, as Rothenberg attempts to do in the way he prints Frank Mitchell's Navajo horse song, in *Shaking the Pumpkin* (pp. 294–95), or as Brian Swann does, in his boldly experimental *Song of the Sky*. At the other extreme, the voice may be flatly conversational, conveying no conscious effort at artistry—no tropes or figures of speech, no echoic phrases, no trace of incremental repetition, no sense of meter or timed pause, no thematic rhythm binding one portion of the discourse to the other, and not so much as a hint of any deep poetry wherein conceptual design is somehow manifest on the vocal surface. In that case, conventional prose might very well suffice to store poetic discourse on the page, as it does, for example, in the passage from *Huckleberry Finn* quoted above. Needed is the recognition, though, that printed prose does not preclude the likelihood that poetry can exist in a given text.

In between the extremes of pure lyric and ordinary conversational speech, however, there are degrees of voice, which is what scholars like Dell Hymes and Dennis Tedlock came to realize, prompting a revived awareness of the place of voice in producing poetry along with a healthy distrust of print to do the job unless used with great care. "Prose has no real existence outside the written page," writes Tedlock. What makes it "unfit for representing spoken narrative is that it rolls on for whole paragraphs at a time without taking a breath: there is no silence in it" (1978, p. xix). Meanwhile, there is all too much silence in verse as it is conventionally displayed in books. Readers must consciously remind themselves that such graphic devices as widened margins, the measured lines, and the empty spaces used to divide stanzas also represent intervals of taking in breath or longer units of pause that mark deeper or more subtle layers of rhythm. They must think consciously about how the poetic voice frames verbal patterns in an effort to describe commensurate patterns external to language on some greater-than-human scale.

I can illustrate how colloquial poetry invokes that transcendent presence, I think, by pointing to features that might at first escape notice in the San Juan Rain God Drama, which was originally recorded as prose (see Laski; Rothenberg: 1972, pp. 214–35).[6] Essentially, the text contains a ritual reenactment of the arrival of life-giving rain gods into a ceremonial kiva, where villagers have gathered to wait as two teasing clowns summon the "Great Ones." Shading their eyes in a mimed effort to gaze into far-off mountains, the clowns look successively to the north, the west, the south, and the east, calling out to each other as they try to spot the oncoming gods. As if coaxing the sacred guests out of the sky, they finally claim to see them, first at far-off "Muddy Water Lake," and then at the less distant "Thunder Lake." They describe how the kachinas make their way closer to the more nearby "Willow Leaf Lake," and then to the still closer "Clearwater Lake." They are "coming out & coming out of it," clear up "to Garbage Gardens" at the outskirts of the village, cry the clowns as the kachinas move through familiar landmarks toward the village (Rothenberg, pp. 220–21).

In *The Tewa World* (pp. 13–28), Alfonso Ortiz explains that by tracking the rain gods across the landscape, the clowns actually verbalize a sacred cosmic conception. According to them, the kachinas circle in from the distance clockwise, intermittently disclosing themselves from a more nearby point in each cardinal direction. With how it is described, their movement coordinates color symbolism with the annual cycle of seasons in an intricate model that ultimately aligns the female earth with the human female. The drama reaches its climax following the arrival of the kachinas when "a young girl about ten years old, dressed in shawl & manta . . . is taken from the crowd" and, by way of symbolic ritual, is inseminated by their chief. "And now yus have consummated yer Man Ceremony!" one of the clowns then says. After the procedure is repeated three more times with three additional girls, the "Silent One" departs as the other kachinas have already done (Rothenberg, p. 322; see also Laski, pp. 54–55). Thus, the drama enacts "contact with the supernatural" in the form of a "dramatic meeting of a people with their gods" (Laski, p. 60).

For all their apparent exuberance and spontaneous irreverence, however, the clowns articulate a sharply conceived, poetically expressed cosmic vision. In making that conjecture, of course, I am limited to the evidence that Laski's English provides. She obviously relied on an interpreter, and nothing in her commentary or her notes suggests that they talked about the Rain God Drama poetically or even that she knew Tewa well enough to appreciate its poetic nuances. Like many anthropologists, she assembled her text as ethnographic data; and although she recognizes its dramatic qualities (pp. 32, 38, 60), she does not think of it as literature or poetry. Nor does she display Tedlock's awareness of how print can be textured to overcome the distortion of translation so as to replicate what is poetic in colloquial speech. Rothenberg's revision resonates more poetically than her text does, but only superficially. If there is deep poetry in the drama, it can be found as readily in Laski's version, too, when read carefully in ritual context.

For instance, the clowns begin telling of the oncoming kachinas when the first one describes a "churning and splashing [and] bubbling" on far-off "Muddy Water Lake." The second one, then, observes a god "sticking his head out," and then "another one coming out, and another one, and another one," specifying four in all before generalizing that "they keep coming out, and keep coming out, and keep coming out" (Laski, p. 43). Whereupon the second clown responds, "More and more of them come out, bringing with them the sacred Cloudflower, bringing with them the power to make rain, the power to raise watermelon, the power to raise musk melon, the power to raise squash, wheat, and corn, the power to hunt deer, the power to hunt buffalo, and they keep coming out with the power to hunt rabbits and the power to kill skunks" (p. 43).

Notice the parallel use of the word *power* in two separate series, one with reference to making rain and growing crops, and a second with reference to hunting game. *Power* is mentioned four times in each sequence, and each sequence designates two categories. The first distinguishes melons from vegetables while the second separates large game from small. The second clown repeats the statement in a slightly abbreviated form when he next reports that the gods "are coming" out of the less distant "Stone Man Lake," to which the first clown replies that he, in turn, sees the same gods emerging from the still closer "Willow Leaf Lake... with their deer killing power, their buffalo killing power, and with their power to raise corn and watermelon and squash and beans," and then out of nearby "Clear Water Lake... with all their thunder and lightning, and rain bringing, with all the goodness of their bean raising, and squash raising, and corn raising, and melon raising, and deer killing, and fox killing, and rabbit killing" (Laski, p. 44).

Each clown, then, adds twice in succession to a series of four parallel reports from four lakes associated with four mountains and four different directions, each recited in closely parallel syntactic units using multiples of four or occasionally three. And while Laski does not indicate Tedlock's precise awareness of the *poesis* underlying such reiterations, or while her English is neither as delicately translated as Tedlock's nor arranged with the same precise graphic care, it still retains a poetic quality—a certain thematic rhythm, if you will—that can be heard. As I say, deep poetry can overcome the distortions of translation.[7] Moreover, the four separate reports verbalize a deeply conceived scheme that may be called poetic in its own right. Taken together, they reflect "specific reference points in the Tewa world" (Ortiz, p. 18) wherein an "ultimate power both male and celestial" is seen to "reach right into the ground to deposit... seeds deep within the earth" (Ortiz, p. 21), whose countervailing female power responds by giving ongoing life.

At some fundamental human level, poetry and religon thereby conjoin in the effort to recognize patterns, to interpret them, and to articulate them and then to verbalize what they mean—linking the patterns of speech and thought with nature's patterns or, if one chooses, the patterns of some broader reality of which human reality is but a portion. As we continue to recognize them and appreciate where they ultimately come from, Native American texts

help us to realize that. Even across awkwardly assembled translations, they do so through the medium of the human voice as it
ranges from the purely lyrical to the naturally colloquial, not only
directing our attention to the important place that poetry occupies
in a culture, but utilizing it as the art which verbalizes understanding and which can summon visions of a greater-than-human
reality even in a purportedly secular age.

Classifying
Poetic Texts
~ *Mode*

The Dramatic Mode

SOMETHING ELSE ABOUT the San Juan Rain God Drama can help in developing a framework for classifying sacred Native American texts, for analyzing and understanding them, for appreciating them on their own indigenous terms, and even for what they can add to the way we read standard European poetic texts. That work is dramatic, by which I mean, first of all, that it usually involves more than one voice as opposed to the single voice of a narrative. While the narrative voice in a work is primarily that of a first-party single speaker recounting to a second-party audience regarding something that took place in the past, the dramatic voice appeals to a third party in anticipation of an immediate response as an audience overhears. If the past is mentioned at all, it pertains to a reality elsewhere, away from the venue of the ensuing dialog.

Because drama represents action taking place now, there is, second of all, a sense of direct involvement in it nonexistent in stories. That immediacy acquires added force in ritual drama, where audiences participate. In hearing narrative, audiences listen to a lone speaker addressing no one in particular, telling exclusively of prior events that occurred someplace apart and remote, sometimes repeating what other characters have said to each other in that world elsewhere. In drama, however, audiences listen and watch as characters seeking a reply address someone in the world immediately at hand. What the characters say places the action directly before onlookers or spectators.

The clowns in the Rain God Drama, for example, eager to bring needed moisture, talk to each other as they summon the gods from distant mountain lakes into the kiva. Occasionally, they talk to spectators in an effort to draw them into the action the clowns instigate. Or they bring selected members onto the stage, as it were, as when four young girls are selected from the audience to be symbolically impregnated by the Great One. In a Navajo ceremony, deities are likewise summoned by a speaker either to help bless an individual or a group or to heal a patient. While onlookers watch, the presiding medicine man, the patient, and various others reenact a traditional event that secures the necessary blessing or cure, which in itself becomes the desired response that dramatic poetry seeks to evoke. The consoling brother in the Iroquois Condolence Ritual has to coax the bereaved one into full recovery before, together, they can install a new council member.

In the third place, because everything in a dramatic work occurs in a staged immediacy, any distinction marking past or future collapses into a dramatic present. To secure that present, spectators and participants alike often gather in a world apart—down a kiva ladder, to a special clearing within a circle of brushwood or stones, inside a longhouse or a ceremonial hogan. To watch our own dramatic productions, we in mainstream Euroamerican culture generally walk under a marquee, pass through a lobby, and present a ticket to an usher at an inner doorway to the separate immediacy of a darkened hall. Presumably, that too is a separate venue where the present absorbs the past—which is invoked only when a speaker elects to do so, always within the framework of the newly fabricated dramatic present. During the course of such a narrative embedding, one or another speaker may refer to a past event to intensify what is currently happening or about to happen.

To identify a work as dramatic, I suggest considering its overall matrix—to borrow a term from mathematics that designates an ordered array of individual units belonging to a set. At its simplest, a matrix, as I use the term here, can be defined as the work's overriding framework or shell, extending from the very opening word to its last—from beginning to proverbial end. With few exceptions, the present tense is used at the outset of a dramatic work with the expectation that any invocation of the past is but one embedded component informing the staged, dramatic present.

If Shakespeare's *Hamlet* is a dramatic matrix overall, lines 59 through 80 in Act I, scene v, contains a narrative embedding within it, for in that passage the ghost tells the prince how he had been murdered in his sleep by Claudius. Characteristic of dramatic literature, the overwrought sentinels Bernardo and Francisco begin the play by making present-tense demands on each other that they identify themselves. "Who's there?" cries the one. "Nay, answer me; stand, and unfold yourself," retorts the other. Thus, whether as readers or members of an audience, we are transported away from any consideration of our own past or future to that well-known rotten Danish world where Elsinore remains shrouded in heavy mist in a tense dramatic present perpetually fixed. Accordingly, the story the ghost tells his son has occurred in a past pertaining to that world, too, rather than to the world outside the theatre which the audiences temporarily quit.

Such an embedding can be placed anywhere in the matrix without altering or displacing its dramatic character, whose chief trait is the immediacy of someone's voice in a world apart addressing someone else or some other-than-human or greater-than-human entity with the expectation of an immediate reply, whether in speech or in kind. The shortest lyrics can be set in a dramatic matrix, and narrative embeddings can be found even in them. Using Margot Astrov's *The Winged Serpent* as a handy reference guide to Native American texts gathered from a wide array of excellent sources all over North America, I point to the Osage selection there (p. 102), entitled "A Warrior's Song from the Mourning Rite," drawn from LaFlésche (pp. 123–24). In that text, a man sets out in mourning for a slain relative. As he wails in the present tense, a world apart from any reader's reality, the kinsman materializes and then invokes the past somewhat in the way that Claudius's ghost does to Hamlet:

Verily, I am a person who has made a god to be his body,
The god of night,
I have made to be my body. . . .

Admittedly, I think of this as a very fleeting, marginally recognizable narrative embedding in a selection from an intensely dramatic mourning ritual. But it is easy to suppose that an apparition of the dead can likewise be fleeting and not ordinarily apprehended.

Translated texts of Plains Indian songs seem to offer an especially rich source of such dramatic material in the lyric voice, where brief narrative embeddings occur swiftly—scarcely more than a fleeting allusion to the past. While they are easy to overlook for the uninitiated reader, they occur frequently: I submit that readers must virtually train themselves to recognize them. Characteristic of what I mean is the lyric titled "Song of a Man Who Received a Vision," which Astrov reproduces (p. 125) from Frances Densmore's ground-breaking study of Teton-Sioux lyric poetry (p. 165). One of many such vision songs, its warrior persona bids his friends, in the present tense, to "behold," then lapses into a past-tense mode to report,

> Sacred I have been made. . . .
> In a sacred manner
> I have been influenced
> At the gathering of the clouds.
> Sacred I have been made. . . .

While the narrative embedding seems admittedly slight because of the imperfective, it is clearly there, however shadowy it appears, as it were. Indeed, that slight, scarcely recognizable modal lapse adds to the visionary quality of what the warrior says.

I suggest that, to be appreciated as a printed work with its own independent poetic force, the poem be read in an essentially dramatic matrix containing a narrative embedding which tells of a visionary happening now completed. Like the sentinels in the opening passage of *Hamlet*, this speaker remains fixed in an ongoing present that the reader must imagine to exist in a world apart, constantly demanding listeners to hear how he has been made sacred the way the ghost will insist on telling how he has been slain. To regard such a text that way adds the dimension of voice to what would otherwise be a mute text. Especially in this electronic reality in which we now live, where print is no longer the pre-dominant medium for experiencing poetry, such a self-conscious reading effort is necessary—all the more so in the case of a printed translation of poetry harvested from a preliterate tribal source presumed to have no established poetic practice.

Look carefully at all seventeen stanzas of Richard Johnny John's printed English rendition of the Seneca Thank-You Prayer and you will notice that while each consists mainly of a narrative embedding describing some particular event in the prior creation of the universe, it opens in the present tense with the statement, "Now so many people that are in this place. . . . " and it ends with the present-tense assertion, "We will give . . . our thanks for it. At this time of day. This is the way it should be in our minds" (Rothenberg, pp. 4–9). Each stanza, in fact, concludes with that present-tense admonition. As if the audience were characters in a play—which is one way of defining ritual drama—the speaker is reminding its members to think and act reverently in keeping with the creator's original intent when he devised a cosmos-wide habitat for humans. Hence the Thank-You Prayer might very well be considered a dramatic matrix consisting largely of narra-tive embeddings whose venue is any one of the ceremonial gath-erings that mark crucial points in the Seneca year.

As with the matrix itelf, a narrative embedding can be colloqui-ally voiced. "Hmmm," says the First Clown early in Rothenberg's version of the Raingod Drama, "t'other day whilst I was walking past the Garbage Gardens who should I see but Flower Mountain (chomp) & she was going out ter gather cowchips. And who would yus think was coming out ter help her?" (Rothenberg, p. 217). Thereupon the clowns shift back to the present tense, reaffirming their immediate desire to bring the rain gods. Similarly, in re-minding his young sibling that the confederacy was founded to bind the Iroquois nations in everlasting peace, the condoling brother lapses narratively into the past tense to remind him in what resembles a colloquial voice, however majestic in its formal-ity, "Now hear, therefore, what [my grandsires] did, all the rules they decided on, which they thought would strengthen the House" (Hale, p. 125).

Or else, just as the dramatic matrix itself can, narrative embeddings can range into the lyrical voice. Washington Matthews refers to a noteworthy example, which suggests that a traditional Navajo healing ceremony can comprise an elaborate poetic composite of voice and mode. Accompanied by a "beating . . . drum, with a peculiar sharp strike like a sudden outburst or explosion," he writes, the medicine man who presides over the Navajo *Mountain Chant* sings during that dramatic ritual about how "'Holy Young Woman sought the gods and found them'" (Matthews: 1897, pp. 462–63). A similarly embedded narrative episode is lyrically recited in the Pawnee Spring Renewal Ceremony, where a group of men and one of women interrupt a dramatic enactment of oncoming rainclouds to take turns singing of how Paruxti the Lightning God once helped to create the earth by drawing power from the sky (Murie, pp. 43–44).

Examples of lyrical narrative embeddings do not seem plentiful, at least at a first unsystematic glance. The phenomenon occurs often enough to warrant careful notice, however, and it remains to carefully survey printed discourse from all tribes if only to determine how adequately the voice-mode scheme applies as an objective, value-neutral way of recognizing and classifying Native American poetry, and of dealing with uncertain categories. From one perspective, for example, so-called autobiographies like John Neihardt's text. *Black Elk Speaks* can be read as a dramatic matrix containing a series of long narrative embeddings consisting mainly of Black Elk's long testimonial, itself interspersed with shorter ones by such others as Fire Thunder, Standing Bear, and Iron Hawk.

Arguably, to be sure, this set of statements dovetails with the above description of the dramatic mode. Black Elk opens by addressing Neihardt directly. "My friend," he begins; "I am going to tell you the story of my life, as you wish." And for the rest of the opening chapter he continues speaking in the present tense, directing Neihardt's attention to the sacred pipe he fills with red willow that they will smoke together, with its four ribbons hanging from the stem, the eagle feather secured to it, and its leather mouthpiece. By so doing, he instills an awareness for eavesdropping readers that Neihardt is but a party in this staged reality he invokes of a world apart. In fact, he describes that world well

enough to permit the reader to imagine its enduring features of
earth and sky, a setting sun, a rising moon. Others in that perpetually present world include the "Grandfather, Great Spirit" (p. 5)
he invokes as he begins to tell of his life and its visions, along with
the deified "Four quarters of the world" (p. 6), and his fellow nar-
rators, who add their stories to his own.

Much of the overall work's considerable poetic power, I might
contend, arises from that carefully developed dramatic setting.
Although consisting largely of the narrative mode, it is manifestly
fixed in a matrix of what one persona in particular says directly to
another. Active readers alert to what Black Elk describes and the
printed simulation of his voice can look on as if from the orchestra
of a theater. Furthermore, it could be argued that Black Elk's
voiced embeddings take on a distinct lyrical quality at crucial
places in his narrative. One notable example among others occurs
in chapter 2, with his description of his great childhood vision.

"Behold him, the being with four legs!" cry the two appari-
tional men who summon the boy to the "world of cloud . . . in the
middle of a great white plain with snowy hills and mountains."
Black Elk thereupon notices a bay horse which, in turn, echoes,
"Behold me! . . . My life-history you shall see." It then turns to
face twelve additional black horses to the west and repeats,
"Behold them! Their history you shall know." The bay then
wheels toward the north and repeats, "Behold," as the youth
overcomes his fright and spies "twelve white horses all abreast."
Such accounts of dancelike verbal movement with its foregrounded commands to "behold" repeated in lines of rhythmic
near-incremental repetition virtually sing out with lyric alacrity
to the reader willing to project beyond the flatly visual silence of
conventionally arranged blocks of prose (Neihardt, p. 23).

While displaying properties unlike those familiar to European
print culture, such as fixed patterns of meter and rhyme, that passage from Neihardt's account, along with scores of others like it,
invites the kind of careful analysis I do not have space to present
here. For now, let me just point to features like the elaborate repetition of syntactical and conceptual components describing his vision of the twelve horses adorned with necklaces of bison hooves
(pp. 22–24); the simpler list of repeated increments describing the

six old men he envisions in the cloud-teepee (p. 25); and even the way in which smaller dramatic units are sub-embedded in the narrative ones like Chinese boxes, in an elaborate structural arrangement that intensifies a kind of thematic rhythm noteworthy in itself. Let me add, too, the suggestion that certain noteworthy Native American autobiographies might work best for readers when considered as dramatic literature whose massive narrative embeddings give them the kind of poetic force that we expect in operatic performances and vocal renditions on the concert stage or the video screen.

Whether lyrical or dramatic, narrative embeddings can vary in length and frequency. Without having looked systematically yet, I think they may help account for the deep dramatic appeal of autobiographical texts such as Black Elk's testimony to John Neihardt as well as with ceremonial ones like those which John Bierhorst has assembled from the Iroquois or James Murie gathered from the Pawnee (see Parks). I also have the impression that they occur relatively more often in Pueblo ceremonies and Iroquois rituals than in Navajo and Pawnee dramatic works, at least among texts with which I am familiar. Furthermore, with the former two tribes they seem more often colloquially voiced, whereas with the latter two they are more apt to be sung.[1] Referring once again to our own mainstream culture, I think of conventionally spoken plays, on the one hand, and opera or musical theater, on the other, or of films and videoplays as opposed to Hollywood musicals like *The Wizard of Oz* or *Singing in the Rain*. In today's abundant, electronically transmitted dramatic poetry, voice can likewise range from the colloquial to the lyrical. That possibility too remains to be explored, just as it remains to match texts which originate in the oral setting of traditional Native American cultures with those that emerge from today's electronic reality and that supplement printed texts—if indeed they have not already begun to displace them.

Sometimes a dramatic matrix may consist of but one voice.[2] What makes it dramatic, then, is that instead of participating in a two-or-more-way encounter like that involving the San Juan clowns and the oncoming rain gods, or instead of addressing a general audience as a storyteller does, the speaker is overheard by the audience as he or she appeals to someone else, expecting a reply either in speech or in kind from the addressee, even though it is not formally part of the work. If indeed they can be considered dramatic, autobiographies like *Black Elk Speaks* represent by and large such single-voiced works, with the anticipated reply being added understanding on the part of whites and at least in certain cases eventual publication (see Krupat: 1983; see also Nichols).

Turning to the familiar English confines of European print tradition, Browning's so-called dramatic monologues provide good illustrations. Read any one of them carefully and you find yourself positing someone who does not actually voice a response on an imaginary stage together with the speaker, and although the reply of the former is not part of the work, what the latter says initiates the dramatic present, leaving you to imagine what the reaction might be. In St. Praxed's church, the dying bishop begs his assembled illegitimate sons to provide him with an opulent tomb there, leaving the reader to wonder if indeed they will honor his final death wish. Probably to no avail, Andrea Del Sarto whines for sympathy to his unfaithful wife before she steps out with a lover. Curiously, that fairly colloquial monologue bears a resemblance to "Ruby," the early Kenny Rogers lyric about a wounded Vietnam vet whose wife is about to "take [her] love to town." In fact, popular song lyrics can likewise be classified as dramatic or narrative. Whether occurring in pop culture, mainstream Anglo-European literate, or Native American poetic tradition, drama can be distinguished from narrative by looking at main verbs for tense markers.

Whereas printed or electronic mainstream dramatic poetry is predominantly secular, single-voiced Native American dramatic poems are more likely to be sacred, although not inevitably so. Secular single-voiced dramatic lyrics from tribal sources are less plentiful than sacred ones. Love songs, for example, appear more infrequently in tribal literature than they do in today's pop culture. "Know the reason of our parting," sings a Dakota wife whose love lyric Natalie Curtis put on paper; "I have watched thee well, faithless one! Clasp my hand and part!" (Curtis, pp. 57, 85).

Sacred examples in which the speaker addresses a deity, a spirit, or even an animal are far more plentiful among all tribes. "You are a spirit, / I am making you a spirit, / In the place where I sit / I am making you a spirit," cries a Chippewa singer whom Frances Densmore recorded over a dying person presumably about to undertake the eschatological journey to a greater-than-human world (Densmore, p. 95). "O Wakonda, you see me a poor man," an Assiniboine warrior begins appealing, in a selection that Astrov reproduces (p. 95) from a set of text originally collected by Edwin Denig (pp. 483–84). "You have left me to linger in hopeless longing," an Osage weaver commences to lament to the spirit of a dead relative in an Osage example that Astrov includes (p. 101) from yet another volume compiled by LaFlésche (pp. 634–35). Once we learn to recognize such sacred poetic statements, in fact, their abundance becomes evident, as even the most cursory look at standard anthologies like those assembled by Astrov, Cronyn, or Rothenberg can show. Native American poetic practice offers a wellspring of sacred dramatic poetry. Among other things, it expands by far the rather limited awareness of religion and religious literature that biblical print tradition allows.

Like the multivoiced sacred dramatic works, the univocal ones can be more purely colloquial, too, as seems to be the case with this one recorded by Truman Michelson (p. 147) from the Fox, who grieve by reciting speeches to the newly deceased: "Now this day you have ceased to see daylight; Think only of what is good. Do not think of anything uselessly. You must think all the time of what is good." Or a single-voice sacred dramatic work might be less purely colloquial, but not entirely lyrical. Perhaps an Eskimo hunting song reworked by Rothenberg is an example, where a hunter appeals to his game to provide him with food: "You, you caribou / yes you," cries the speaker in a dramatic lyric that Rothenberg reworks from an older translation from the Inuit; "See, I'm holding in my hand / the reindeer moss you're dreaming of— / so delicious, yum, yum, yum— / Come, caribou, come" (p. 43; see also pp. 350–52). In fact, anthologies such as those compiled by Rothenberg or Astrov are full of such monologues, sacred more often than secular. Consciously inquiring of the text about which is which can help a reader appreciate a given selection. Who is speaking and to whom? a greater-than-human spiritual entity? If so, does the circumstance call for the deliberately stylized verbal patterns characteristic of the lyrical voice? At the very least, raising such questions can help a reader approaching the poem from outside the culture of its origin make distinctions that are self-evident to listeners from within the culture. Such questions can encourage a second, more careful look at a poem that at first seems flat, prosaic, or remotely unappealing.

The predominance of sacred dramatic poetry, whether single-voiced or multivocal, draws attention to the poetics of prayer, which, in general, can be considered a subgenre of dramatic poetry wherein a greater-than-human or other-than-human reality is addressed—a largely unexplored sector of poetics that begs for added consideration (see Reichard: 1944; Gill: 1974, for two rare but excellent examples; see also Beck, Walters, and Francisco, pp. 35–45). That, in turn, leads to ways of classifying sacred Native poetry and using it to get beyond fatuous generalizations like "Indians live close to the land," or that they are spiritual people. Such bland statements remain useless without concrete examples or systematic exploration of what they might actually mean. Looking exclusively at material culture does not really help since physical artifacts do not articulate in the way that language can. And reading contemporary literature by Native American writers (most of whom are of mixed blood and products largely of creative writing courses and mainstream culture) does not provide a complete understanding any more than reading Dante while knowing nothing about New Testament culture does. Nor is the full range of any tribal culture fully explained by simply calling the Lakota or the Mohawks victims, however sympathetically. To dismiss them merely as that without any detailed, curious regard for their various conceptions of the sacred is to add to that victimization in an insidious way. The fullest possible measure of that regard, I contend, comes from the recognition that Native Americans are among the world's peoples who have traditionally maintained a deep and abiding dialog with a greater-than-human reality. As well as any physical or cultural anthropologist, the literary critic can explore the dramatic depths of that relationship.

The Narrative Mode

LET ME SAY first of all that I consider any narrative potentially poetic, whether recited orally or in print and to any degree along the lyrical-voice continuum. Initiating a brief introductory discussion of narrative, however, is no easy task because so very much has been written about it, ranging from histories of the novel and discussions of the short story, the folk or fairy tale, and even myths and legends to the newer theoretical interest among scholars from all disciplines in narratively framed verbal artifacts as varied as film, autobiography, and personal accounts. I cannot pretend to be an authority on narrative, especially when writings about it have proliferated so. Nor can I easily point to a single work or a concise set of titles that might launch a systematic survey of the study of narrative, beyond recommending an opening look into *The Princeton Encyclopedia of Poetry and Poetics*, which identifies species of narrative while supplying useful references and a summary bibliography.

For now, however, let me limit my preliminary discussion of narrative to some very basic distinctions largely of my own devising, to an occasional quote, and to a few speculations or tentative observations applicable mainly to Native American examples. That way I can perhaps construct some guidelines for distinguishing that mode from the dramatic, all by way of initiating a taxonomy of Native American texts that emerge in print from traditional oral sources. Bear in mind, though, that the following comments are preliminary remarks awaiting greater refinement. Furthermore, no generalization made below precludes exceptions. I invite them, in fact, especially if they accompany careful, open-minded consideration.

To tell a story is to attempt poetic creativity. Zumthor reports that "around 1930, a Canadian Eskimo (or rather an Inuit) confided in his memoirs that telling tales is the stuff of life" (p. 38). Storytelling is that fundamental, I agree—but I would shape that nameless Inuit's statement into the broader assertion that poetry-making of any sort is the stuff of life, especially of social life, which demands artistry to reach its highest effect. I grant, though, that traditionally emplaced narratives underlie more refined efforts at poetry-making such as short songs or highly stylized prayers and chants, mindful that the primary medium of poetry is the human voice, whether solo or in concert with others.

If dramatic poetry is multivoiced, or where a single speaker in a dramatic monologue makes a statement in anticipation of a response from someone else or from some other-than-human entity, a narrative poem ultimately comes from the voice of a single storyteller directly addressing a specific audience without expecting it to issue a particular reply. A seasoned or professional storyteller, whether a print-oriented novelist, a respected Navajo singer, or a West African griot, addresses a reading audience or an assembled group primed to follow a sequence of events leading to a particular outcome. Amy Shuman, who is what I am tempted to call a storyist (i.e., one who examines narratives in their performance context) rather than an exclusively print-oriented literary critic, deals with narrative very fundamentally. According to her, it can be defined "as extended turns at talk in which utterances are sequentially organized"; as "the recapitulation of past experiences in the order in which they are believed"; or "as proposing a world other than that inhabited by the listeners" (Shuman, p. 24; see also Labov: 1972, pp. 359–60; and Jason). Misia Landau provides an even more basic definition when she says that "an entire narrative can be represented as a string of slots, each open to a variety of alternatives" (1991, p. 4).

There are many such definitions, however, and I leave it to readers to harvest enough to acquire a working understanding of the term within or outside of any particular theoretical approach or critical perspective. Here, though, let me summon one trait that narratives seem to have in common as opposed to dramatic works. In reciting events that have occurred successively at some prior time and hence generally placing verbs in the past tense, the storyteller expects no direct reply from any individual person or transhuman entity so long as he or she is addressing an audience instead of a particular individual outside the story's framework.

In some cases, the performer might first seek approval to begin reciting. "SON'AHCHI," begins Andrew Peynetsa in Dennis Tedlock's transcribed English version of "The Boy and the Deer," whereupon his listeners reply, "Ee———so." Following a second such exchange, he then begins his story. "Long ago," he says, "there were villages at Heshokta, and up on the Prairie-Dog Hills the deer had their home" (Tedlock: 1978, p. 3) Placing his story in a time long ago with the immediate use of such forms as the perfective mode and the simple past in the very first sentence, he establishes its narrative framework, which calls for the continued use of the past tense and no further response from the audience.

Within that framework, however, the storyteller can quote something that does require a reply, but that response comes from a character within the story and must fit the narrative scheme. In one of the story's many such dramatic embeddings, when the narrator of "The Boy and the Deer" repeats the boy's question, "WHERE IS MY MOTHER?" the audience is not expected to answer; rather, the performer himself repeats the boy's uncle's response: "She is in a room on the fourth story down weaving basket plaques" (Tedlock: 1978). A longer interlude of exchanges requiring a narrator to stretch his or her own voice to simulate other voices occurs when Coyote taunts Tábaastíín dine'é the Otter People until they tear him to shreds in *Diné bahane'* (Zolbrod: 1984, pp. 147–53). Whether inserted in longer narratives or told as separate stories, trickster narratives are likely to be full of dramatic embeddings. Thereby they provide opportunities to vary voice and body movement which performers and audiences alike enjoy. Navajos often use words abundant in nasal vowels when Coyote speaks, in order to insert a comical whine in what he says, for instance.

Just as a dramatic poem can contain any number of narrative embeddings, repeated by one actor or another who might speak in the past tense to recite something that belongs in the matrix, so a narrative matrix can include any number of dramatic embeddings wherein someone in the story speaks in anticipation of a response from some other character. The printed narratives in mainstream literary tradition contain numerous comparable instances— belonging to the broad category of dialog. Twain's *Huckleberry Finn* offers one noteworthy example, highlighted by the author's prefatory explanation that the work contains "a number of dialects," including "the Missouri negro dialect; the extremest form of the backwoods South-Western dialect; the ordinary 'Pike-

County' dialect; and four modified varieties of this last." Twain obviously wanted his readers to notice his storyteller's effort to reproduce the voices of his characters authentically. "The shadings have not been done in a hap-hazard fashion, or by guesswork," he goes on to say; "but pains-takingly, and with the trustworthy guidance and support of personal familiarity with these several forms of speech" (Twain: 1985, p. xvii). Whether spoken or reproduced in writing, all voices are filtered through the narrator's own solo omni-voice. When other voices are reproduced that way, the speaker may gesture and mime or alter vocal qualities such as pitch and tone to strengthen the impression that a dialogue is taking place in a dramatic embedding.[3]

As I have suggested, Tedlock's English text of "The Boy and the Deer" offers a narrative matrix rich in dramatic embeddings whose intensity mounts with each respective dialogue—first between the deer mother and the kachinas or between her and the boy; and then in the subsequent exchange between the boy and his real mother before he takes his life (Tedlock: 1978, pp. 6–7, 16–20, 24–27). When looked at closely, in fact, the story's suspense grows with each exchange, and each bears careful analysis to discover how configurations of diction and syntax in the respective dramatic embeddings help to sustain interest, increase suspense, add pathos, or contribute other effects that make well told stories compelling. The careful placement of those embeddings can even add to the thematic rhythm in a narrative work, especially when they are evenly spaced.

Navajo stories are likewise full of dramatic interludes that increase their effectiveness (see Zolbrod: 1992b). I found it particularly challenging to reconstruct the quarrel between *Áltsé hastiin* the First Man and his wife *Alté asdzáá* the First Woman in assembling my English textual version of the Navajo creation cycle (see Zolbrod: 1984, pp. 58–59). After reading several other written interpretations, listening to a number of recited accounts, and talking with men and women about male–female relationships in everyday Navajo life, I decided to try to use a simple but formal diction to express the comic anger of that sacred couple without trivializing it, and employed a rapid exchange of short, crisply repetitive declarations. Similarly, in the dramatic embedding which tells of their reconciliation, I wanted to make the *Asdzáá nádleehé* the Changing Woman's demands upon *Jóhonaa'éí* the Sun convincingly intense (Zolbrod: 1984, pp. 272–75). Having listened often enough to spoken narratives, I had gained an awareness of how, among other devices, I recognized that her demands could be expressed in multiples of fours, ranging from four successive declarative sentences parallel in structure to single declarative sentences with simple verbs presiding over four direct objects or two sets of two objects each.

Seasoned storytellers, I had discovered, maintain tight control over syntax that way—so that the voices of all characters can be filtered effectively through the master-voice of a single speaker. Grammatical structure is always at work where dramatic exchanges are embedded. In the discourse of oral storytelling, phrases can be inverted to create a comic but dignified effect when a particular character is speaking, or patterns of syntax can be altered slightly with each repetition to add semantic fervor in something said. Any storyteller can adjust his or her narrative by filling it with or emptying it of dramatic embeddings on one occasion but not on another, which helps to make live storytelling an elastic art in ways in which novels or other printed narratives cannot be. Oral storytellers, of course, enjoy the benefits of that kind of elasticity; once a story is written, however, such options no longer exist for the print-oriented storyteller. A story told in print is recited once and for all; an orally recited narrative can be refashioned again and again to suit each audience. Much of the pleasure of hearing the same story told and retold in the company of very different audiences comes from waiting to see how it might be recited this time, or how and to what degree its dramatic embeddings are altered by the narrator's multifarious voice. In the storytelling practices of any oral culture, dramatic embeddings, whether narrative or colloquial, provide a similarly wide spectrum of kinetic options, which adds to the dynamic of live narration. Zumthor remarks that in an oral performance nonlinguistic forms take on added importance, since the body becomes a narrative instrument that can rival the influence of language on top of drawing attention to it. "The body is both the physically individualized body of each one of the persons engaged in the performance," he writes, "and the harder to discern but ever so real body of collectivity such as is made manifest in emotional reactions and common movements" (p. 62).

Whether instigated by the storyteller or among members of a live audience, on the nondynamic page his or her kinetic options are ordinarily reduced to syntax, to word selection, and the few choices that conventional print graphics allow, such as quotation marks and the new paragraphing of each separate speaker's contribution to the dramatic embedding. Once written down, final redactive choices cannot vary without creating a "new edition." The disadvantage of trying to duplicate body language in an alphabetical text lies in the indelibility of print and in its silence. Any given misjudgment, no matter how small, is permanent. Techniques cannot be refined with each telling, nor adjusted for a particular audience. Print does not easily recreate the physical impact of a storyteller's shifting eye contact, the unexpected shout or the sudden whisper, the wide sweep of a right arm or a left, the way he or she can become a large speaker in a dramatic embedding by rising on the balls of his feet or throwing back her shoulders.

Storytelling and theater display other differences, though, besides that of the storyteller's single-voiced appeal directly to an audience as opposed to the dramatic persona's appeal to a third party. To my mind, what distinguishes a narrative matrix from its dramatic counterpart most, at least in Native American storytelling, is its removal to a far-off past and very often a sacred one. Whereas the action in drama is immediate because it summons elements of the sacred from a time and place elsewhere into the arena of the dramatic present—whether a kiva, a hogan, a plaza, or a longhouse—narrative transports an audience to a world elsewhere in time and place alike. According to Tedlock, the Zunis call that distant world the *inoote* or the long-ago—before "the introduction of objects and institutions... belonging to the period of European contact" (1983, p. 160).

Sometimes the removal to that past becomes a veritable shamanic venture; you can actually watch as a performer transports him or herself to that venue often more distant in terms of time than in space. Navajo singers and storytellers I have watched do that adeptly. Almost as a matter of course, they can deliver an audience to an illusory world elsewhere, especially in a ceremonial hogan where a sandpainting has been painstakingly assembled to attract various supernaturals and spirit-people. To readers who have never actually witnessed a performing poet undertaking such a transformation, I like to cite a photograph of a Navajo singer during a Coyoteway ceremony recorded by Luckert. He sits cross-legged on the hogan floor, his eyes closed, his head tilted back and upward as he leans slightly forward, rattle in hand, obviously singing with enough intensity to place his facial muscles in sharp relief. Just looking suggests that spiritually he is elsewhere in time, and having heard and read lyrics such as those he is singing I know that to be the case (Luckert: 1979, p. 39). An effective storyteller can likewise summon his or her audience to that distant world, in sharp contrast with the here-and-now world which personae in a drama bring to an audience fixed in an ongoing present.

By one way of reckoning, two different types of narrative are set in that remote storytelling world: what the Zunis call *chimiky'ky'anakowa*, which "is regarded as literally true," and the *telapnaawe*, which is considered fiction. The former "accounts for most of the major features of social organization," and belongs "to a period when the world was 'soft'" enough to be shaped according to a shared conception of the way things now are. The latter take place slightly later "in a world which had already hardened, though it was still not quite like the present world" (Tedlock: 1983, pp. 159–60). With its soft, rapidly changing land and skyscape, *Chimiky'ana'kowa* can be associated—at least loosely—with what Clark Wissler calls "myths of cultural and other origins." In the first place, he says, "such narratives account for certain conditions in humanity and nature and certain folk practices, which helps to explain why they are considered to be true. In the second place, the origins and transformations are primary rather than secondary parts of the narrative" (p. 15). By that I take Wissler to mean that they motivate the story and are not incidental to it, the way the soft, ever-changing world projected in Tedlock's Zuni origin story motivates its various characters to act as they do. Moreover, that constant flow of creation and transition remains central to the story and adds a sensation of ongoing change to the separate world to which the storyteller removes his audience. Notice, for example, how rapidly the unformed underworld inhabitants progress through their dark, subterranean domain in Tedlock's printed English version of the Zuni "Beginning, Part I," once the Ahayuuta brothers descend to guide them to the earth's sunlit surface, and how they are at once transformed from shapeless, seedlike creatures to fully developed humans possessing arms and legs, hands and feet, fingers and toes (Tedlock: 1978, pp. 225–71).

While Tedlock cautions that "some narratives are hard to classify according to this [chimiky'ana'kowa-telapnaawe] dichotomy" (1983, p. 160; see also 1968, pp. 214–15), some inferences can be drawn about how the two narrative types overlap and how they might differ. Whether fully soft or beginning to harden, the inoote is a time when communication takes place between all beings, human or otherwise. Thus, the Ahayuuta twins can explain to the subterranean prehuman creatures they visit why they have descended into that underground domain of the soft world of the chimiky'ana' kowa described in "The Beginning" (Tedlock: 1978, p. 234). And in the more recent, hardened world of the telapnaawe, the deer mother in "The Boy and the Deer" can likewise talk freely to her adopted son (Tedlock: 1978, pp. 24–26).

On one hand, the earlier, softer long-ago cosmos is not yet fully formed, though, nor are the shapes of objects and creatures yet fixed. This truly is a time of beginnings, which is what the term chimiky'ana'kowa literally means (Tedlock: 1983, p. 235). The fresh earth still has the "smell" of "ozone," or "K'oli," the "smell of lightning." The Ahayuuta brothers swiftly materialize out of foamy rivulets made when a heavy rainfall hits alkaline soil (Tedlock: 1978, pp. 226–27). Once they emerge from below, the shapeless underground creatures shed their mossy skin, and the webbing which binds their hands and feet is immediately undone. They change shape to become humans (pp. 265–66) in a gesture belonging to the "mythical times" Luckert speaks of when all living things enjoyed the "primeval kinship . . . of essential continuity" which he calls "prehuman flux" (1975: p. 133). These are the narratives that account for reality as it is commonly seen now.

In the "Boy and the Deer," on the other hand, and with other examples of *telapnaawe* in *Finding the Center*, the action occurs in a fully made cosmos. Softness prevails only residually in the ongoing communication that takes place between humans and nonhumans and in the way that animals and sometimes deities can be summoned to intervene in human affairs, as they do in a narrative like "The Woman and the Man" (Tedlock: 1978, pp. 85–132). The Apaches, meanwhile, seem to refine further the temporal distinction implied by separating the *inoote* from a more recent time with greater precision than the Zuni division allows. They classify traditional narratives as *godiyihgo* or "myth" and *agodzaahí* or "historical tale," more or less in alignment with the Zuni *chimiky'ana'kowa* and *telapnaawe*; but they also identify two categories of time, respectively, for the two types of narrative—*godiyaaná'* "the beginning," and *doo'áníí* or "the long ago" (see Basso, pp. 114–19).

As print-oriented non-Indians continue learning about North American tribal practices, additional discoveries will emerge about ways of classifying poetic narratives temporally. For now, however, the Zuni classification is useful because it can be applied somewhat to narratives of other tribes and even to those of Europe and Anglo-America, at least generally. The Bible and Classical Greece have produced *chimiky'ana'kowa*, respectively, in the first two chapters of Genesis and Hesiod's *Theogeny*. That recognition allows readers to begin thinking of them as narratives rooted in orality among tribal cultures with seminal, long-lasting influence. A "soft," unformed, chaotic mass seems fundamental to any effort in describing preternatural beginnings. "The earth was without form and void, and darkness was upon the face of the deep," reads the second verse of Genesis. "First of all came Chaos," says Hesiod as he follows his opening invocation with the narrative portion of his *Theogeny* (Lattimore, p. 130). "God created matter out of nothingness in order that his power might be manifested," repeats the poet who begins the Persian epic of kings with an account of cosmic creation (Levy, p. 1).

The soft world of the Zuni *inoote* thus finds its counterpart in God's swift seven-day creation of the "heavens and the earth," while chapters in Genesis and many of the subsequent narratives in the Old Testament take readers back to a more recent past when the world is still soft enough for voices to call to Noah, a burning bush to speak to Moses, or the Holy Spirit to mediate between God and Mary. What helps make that poetry sacred to this day among practicing Christians is that it continues to define much of their culture. Hesiod's world is similarly that of the early, softer *inoote* of the *chimiky'ana'kowa*. In it, "Erebos, the dark, and black Night" is born from Chaos, and "Gaia's first born" is "one who matched her every dimension, Ouranos, the starry sky" (Lattimore, p. 130). Any poetic effort to trace Persian royalty to its roots perforce begins with a cosmic history. On the other hand, the Homeric world has hardened somewhat, but is still soft enough for Pallas Athene to appear before Achilles or Odysseus or for oracular statements to govern choices that humans make.

Traditional Native American narratives have found their way into print, thanks to early bulletins and reports of the Bureau of American Ethnography and to more recent translators like Dennis Tedlock, Dell Hymes, Julian Rice, and Elaine Jahner. Thus, numerous alphabetical stories exist from among many tribes comparable to what the Zuni call the *inoote*, which likewise tell of soft worlds and hard—*chimiky'ana'kowa* and *telapnaawe*. The Iroquois story of a Turtle Island expanding to become the earth that Good Mind and his grandmother further shape is one example; and as a kind of protonarrative it informs other poetic events in the ceremonial life of that people. Notice, for example, that the still malleable earth and its surrounding cosmos change shape as completely in the Seneca Thank-You Prayer as it does in its parent story, "The Woman Who Fell from the Sky" (see above, pp. 24–25), although the former is essentially a short dramatic lyric while the latter is a long narrative.

In "Thank You," we thus see how narrative can be embedded and compacted into what then becomes a dramatic lyric. In much the same way, for example, the combined New Testament nativity story is compacted into a dramatic lyric like the standard Christmas carol, "God Rest Ye Merry Gentlemen." Throughout the corpus of Native American poetry we can find numerous examples of that kind of compression, wherein a *chimiky'ana'kowa* can be abbreviated and then embedded for another kind of occasion, which might then be recorded on the page as another entire work. In that manner, creation stories remain fundamental poetic works, feeding narratives and plays alike, whether lyrically or colloquially. Embedded in a Tlingit speech to commemorate the dead, which Astrov records, for example, is a summary of that tribe's *chimiky'ana'kowa* (pp. 290–92; or see Swanton: 1909, pp. 374–77).

Similarly, and characteristic of lyric prayers from other tribes, a Zuni prayer of infant dedication embeds a compressed reference to the narrative account of how the Sun Father summoned people from the deep underground to populate the earth. "Now this is the day," it begins in the present tense, which most often signals the dramatic mode, and thus contines:

> Our child,
> Into the daylight
> You will go out standing.

Then it lapses into the past-tense narrative embedding which refers to a ten-day, postnatal waiting period now nearing an end before the child is to be presented to the procreative sun, whose offspring originally guided today's human beings from within the earth:

> Preparing for your day,
> We have passed our days.
> When all your days were at an end,
> When eight days were past,
> Our sun father
> Went in to sit down at his sacred place
> And our night fathers,
> Having come out standing to their sacred place,
> Passing a blessed night
> (Astrov, pp. 231–32; Bunzel, p. 635)

The principle of narrative embeddings in lyric matrices becomes important, in fact, because, among other things, it allows all the more readily the recognition of *chimiky'ana'kowa* story-telling as a force fundamental to all sorts of poetic activity, ranging from stories and songs that entertain to ceremonies that invoke greater-than-human power. Again illustrating from the more familiar poetic counterparts abundantly found in Western culture, think of the manner in which Hesiod's *Theogeny* is compressed into passages embedded in Pindar's odes, how the opening chapters of Genesis are deeply embedded in a fairly familiar song like "Morning Has Broken," or how tightly impacted narrative embeddings function to summon God in standard Protestant hymns.

Narrative episodes from many other tribes can just as easily be considered *chimiky'ana'kowa*, such as those in *Diné bahane': The Navajo Creation Story*, where the seven sacred mountains are created to mark the world's boundaries in all three dimensions or where the sun is carefully positioned in the sky so that the earth is neither too warm nor too cold (Zolbrod: 1984, pp. 86–92). Or consider a very striking passage in Matilda Coxe Stevenson's printed English version of the Zia cosmogony, where the primal, spiderlike deity *Sus'sistinako* transforms empty chaos into a full and orderly sphere by webbing a line "from north to south," crossing it "midway from east to west," then placing "two little parcels north of the cross line" which "hatch" from them to become two life-bearing females whose progeny go on to shape a world and instigate subsequent cosmic creation wherein humans can come into existence and function (Stevenson: 1894, pp. 26–27, 32 fn). Thus, out of that softest, most unformed mass evolves life as presently characterized by current strictures and mores of clan and family.

Such episodes belong to the vast body of what I call cosmogenic narratives. Those stories convey the basic perceptions of reality that distinguish culture from culture and tribe from tribe, and they set forth the values that predicate each group's social organization. As someone on familiar terms with people from places like the Allegany Seneca reservation, the Navajo *Dinébekayah*, or such Pueblo villages as San Juan or Zia, I often hear specific references to those stories in everyday conversation, especially to justify an attitude or to explain a relationship, whether with another person or with some nonhuman component, either abstract or concrete. That, I think, helps in understanding why Tedlock remarks that with its soft world in rapid change the *chimiky'ana'kowa* "accounts for most... major features of... social organization," and why "it is regarded as literally true" (Tedlock: 1983, p. 160). A similarly applied frame of reference also accounts for some of the functions of our own Genesis narrative, not necessarily as prescribed doctrine (although some readers would render it doctrinaire), but as poetic narrative that helps shape ongoing values in Western society, even today when the movement toward secularization appears to be intensifying.

Likewise, among all tribes there are numerous *telapnaanawee*, or stories, which take place in the hardened phase of what the Zunis call the *inoote*, where cosmic and earthly creation is complete but where communication still occurs between the human and the greater-than-human. Trickster stories often fall into this category. So do certain etiological tales, such as the Navajo chantway narratives, which tell how various illnesses and afflictions first originated and how their respective cures were devised. To be sure, Coyote is a major participant in creating the soft world of the Navajo *chimiky'ana'wa* as well. In one recorded sequence, for example, he helps to divide each day into periods of daylight and darkness (see Wyman: 1970, pp. 369–77). In another, he scatters stars in the sky helter-skelter because he lacks the patience to adorn it with carefully assembled constellations (Zolbrod: 1984, pp. 92–94). Once the world hardens into its present shape, though, Coyote remains a major actor in *telapnaawe* as well—not only in Navajo tradition, but in those of other tribes—sometimes to the detriment of humankind and sometimes helpfully (see Luckert: 1979, pp. 191–223; see Rothenberg, pp. 89–94). Other supernaturals and animals interact with people in the hardening world of the *telapnaawe*, too, where a major trait remains the communication that can occur between humans and other-than-human beings. In one episode of the creation cycle, *Yoolgai asdzáá* the White Shell Woman relays a message to a whole group of people through a child's dream (Zolbrod: 1984, p. 293); in another, *Asdzáá nádleehé* the Changing Woman speaks outright to a human group, instructing them to migrate eastward to join a larger contingent of fellow *nihookáá' dineé*, or earth surface people (Zolbrod: 1984, p. 317).

The identification of the *inoote* brings a refreshing perspective to alphabetical poetic traditions like those of Europe and the so-called cradle of civilization in the Middle East. As I suggest, *chimiky'ana'kowa* come out of European and Semitic cultures, too, notably from the Bible and Greek tradition, as well as from those of the Far East. No culture is without such narratives, although if we think of them only as myths or as religious texts in the narrower and more sectarian way that we often invoke religion, we minimize their importance as poetry and as sacred works in the broader framework of the ongoing human attempt to forge links with something that transcends human limitations.

There are vestiges of such an expansively sacred effort in Carlo Ginzburg's remarkable chronicle of a simple Italian miller who was persecuted by the Inquisition because he insisted upon reciting fragments of what must have been a pre-Christian Indo-European cosmogenic narrative. In fact, I consider Carl Sagan's *Cosmos* an interesting contemporary example of a modern-day *chimiky'ana'kowa*. Transmitted electronically as well as in print, it replaces the kiva or the longhouse with the home video screen (see Rodgers and Zolbrod). All modern-day efforts to postulate the cosmic and terrestrial origins show some of the traits of *chimiky'ana'kowa* so long as they take on the linear form of narrative. Some of them, like Sagan's version of *Cosmos*, exhibit poetic qualities, although it remains to determine where they fit on the lyric-to-colloquial voice continuum. Some of them may be less poetic. In either case, however, we have no reason to suppose that empirical science or any sort of positivistic methodology has stripped humankind of the need to account for the other-than-human causality of life and the classification of its myriad forms. The details of such narratives will change from culture to culture and across time's expanse, but the human need to tell the story will never diminish; nor will the human community ever lapse in its need to transact its visions poetically, whether by way of the immediate voice, the use of print, or electronic technology.

Vestiges of European *telapnaawe* also abound in the alphabetical cultures of Euroamerica, ancient and contemporary alike. They survive richly within the framework that Jacob Grimm and his brother explored and among the sources that Hans Christian Andersen tapped, or in such works as the Icelandic *Volsungsaga* and the Welsh *Mabinogion* and its accompanying Arthurian lore. It all boils down to a fundamental principle: poetry antedates print, and it represents an early struggle to associate the human with larger forces perceived in the *inoote*, the definition of which I would now expand to include that time prior to modern ways of recording history or verifying measurement, or even to the invention of conditions of softness associated with such a time. Especially in their narrative embeddings, Shakespeare's comedies and romances thus invoke characteristics of *telapnaawe*, with their recourse to Prospero's magic in *The Tempest*, or the presence of such creatures as Caliban and Ariel, or with the coming to life of Hermione's statue in *The Winter's Tale*. The Faust of Marlowe and Berlioz and Thomas Mann belongs to the not yet totally hard world of the later phase of the *inoote*, as does Byron's Childe Harold and Keats's Endymion. I am no aficionado of contemporary fantasy and science fiction colloquial narratives, but it seems to me that in many of them the still somewhat soft world of the *inoote* is being constantly invoked or reinvented. By its very nature, it seems, humankind must inevitably strive to maintain contact with a greater-than-human reality, summoning an intellectual curiosity and sophisticated artistry that poetry articulates in its special verbal way.

I mention all of that not to subordinate traditional Native American sacred narrative to the more prestigious European poetic traditions, nor to assert any inevitable superiority of alphabetical poetry over what is stored in the memory and delivered orally. Rather, I do so to strengthen my broader position that sacred tribal texts which Native American cultures yield can expand our appreciation of European narratives and related poetic works, which still go a long way toward explaining the underpinnings of social organization brought here from the so-called Old World. Beyond that, Native American poetic artifacts recovered from the *inoote* can redirect awareness that great poetry, whatever its origins, is fundamentally sacred in ways that Judeo-

Christian and Islamic sectarianism cannot alone encumber. I realize, of course, that such assertions as these are widely speculative
and almost too boldly general. Nonetheless, I like to think that
they point to areas of further investigation or exploration that
promise to dignify all poetic activity, including that of Native
Americans. Such an experiment is worth attempting, at any rate,
even if it calls for extended amplification or major revision of
what I tentatively project here.

FIVE

Toward a
Taxonomy of
~ Texts

THE POETIC VOICE can sound lyrical or colloquial by degree. A given poem—say one in blank verse by Maya Angelou or William Carlos Williams—may be somewhat colloquial. Meanwhile, a church hymn or one of Coleridge's or Wordsworth's *Lyrical Ballads* may be purely lyrical. John Donne's poems show a masterful technique of making tightly structured metrical rhyme sound colloquial, which locates them somewhere in the middle of what I call the lyric–colloquial voice continuum. Thus voice is a matter of degree. Mode, on the other hand, occurs in a more absolute state. A work's overall matrix is either narrative or dramatic, merging only insofar as a passage characteristic of one can be embedded within a larger passage exhibiting traits of the other.

Accordingly, it may be possible to classify any text according to the dual criteria of voice and mode. That possibility may apply to all poetry; but it can certainly help readers sort through printed discourse originally drawn from Native American oral traditions, which thus endure as part of a vibrant, ongoing oral poetic practice. Rooted more evidently in the sound of the human voice manifestly at work in relating to a sacred or greater-than-human reality, that material allows the scrutiny of poetry as performance in ways that Europe's written poetic legacy does not as easily permit. Someone somewhere first voiced the prototype of a given text before its words were written: someone issued a statement or an outcry and expected a reply in an effort to effect some sort of change; or else someone told a story about an erstwhile change. A poetic voice is manifestly at work, even though at first eclipsed by the silence of the page, creating drama or telling a story. Thereby, I relent to voice as well as to mode in edifying my contention that Native American peoples have produced significant poetry which can stimulate a broadly applicable classification by voice and mode.

With its seemingly cadenced lines and majestic formality, *The Iroquois Condolence Ritual* assumes an apparently chantlike voice that makes it fairly lyrical. At least that is the impression created by the stanzaic units of Hale's transcription of the Onondaga version he acquired from John Buck, or Skanawati, to cite the council name of Hale's major informant (p. 41). Readers of a translation cannot be sure that such a work is performed lyrically, although Hale's use of stanzaic print serves as a reliable indication, even if his English does not adequately represent the qualities of Onondaga song. In several places he arranges his transliterations syllable by syllable, most notably in reproducing a preliminary interlude for which he lists the title, "At the Wood's Edge." These four consecutive stanzas are arranged that way, for example (pp. 119–21).

5.

Ka rhe tyon ni.	The broad woods.
Ogh ska wa se ron hon.	Grown up to bushes again.
Gea di yo.	Beautiful plain.
O nen yo deh.	Protruding stone.
De se ro ken.	Between two lines.
Te ho di jen ha ra kwen.	Two families in a long-house,
Ogh re kyon ny.	(Doubtful.) [one at each end].
Te yo we yen don.	Drooping Wings.

6.

Ka ne sa da keh.	On the hill side.
Onkwi i ye de.	A person standing there.
Wegh ke rhon.	(Doubtful)
Kah ken doh hon.	"
Tho gwen yoh.	"

7.

De ya oken	The Forks.
Jo non de seh.	It is a high hill.
Ots kwe ra ke ron.	Dry branches fallen to the ground.
Ogh na we ron.	The springs.

8.

Ka rho wengh ra don.	Taken over the woods.
Ka ra ken.	White.
De yo he ro.	The place of flags (rushes).
De yo swe ken.	Outlet of the river.
Ox den ke.	To the old place.

Combined, the stanzas contain twenty-three lines. Twelve of them consist of four syllables, which may indicate something of a standard length—seemingly determined by sound alone since they display no semantic or syntactical norm when translated into English. Five of the remaining lines contain three syllables, while four of the others consist of five, leaving two which contain six and seven syllables, respectively.

Standard four-syllable lines occur consecutively, while lines longer or shorter than that never do. That feature adds to the possibility of a chantlike lyric voice in an actual performance. One cannot be sure, of course, without actually hearing the work recited, or without some explicit description of what it sounds like. But when readers have an opportunity to pause and examine a text such as that which Hale provides in producing a bilingual rendering, they can monitor the print graphics as closely as possible to at least gain an approximation, such as I have tried to do here. If nothing else, such a close visual look serves as a reminder that the text originated in a distinct voice, a different language, a different culture, and a medium of production far different from that of the printed page as produced by a Wordsworth or an Emily Dickinson.

Meanwhile, because it consists primarily of declarations by an elder, condoling brother to a younger bereaved one, the *Condolence Ritual* also fits into a dramatic matrix, even though it contains scattered narrative embeddings, especially in passages that refer back to the more hardened time of the *inoote*, when the confederacy was formed under the visionary inspiration of Dekanawida and the forceful oratory skill of Hayenwatha. So that work can be considered a lyrical narrative, although readers of an English textual version must remain aware of being far removed from the oral prototype. By recognizing the work as dramatic, however, they can arm themselves with a reminder that while print has removed them from the original, it is possible to imagine the respective voices of the allegorical dialogue. Beyond that, it becomes possible to picture the action by reading the text with added care and by examining ethnographic descriptions by scholars like Hale or Parker.

The San Juan Rain God Drama likewise consists of a dramatic matrix. In that work the two clowns alternately address each other, those present in the kiva, and the kachinas whom they summon. A careful look at both versions of the available translation of that text produces the impression that their statements belong to a fairly colloquial voice, although they occasionally appear to speak with songlike lyricism. Thanks to Laski's orthography, which Rothenberg pretty much follows, readers can recognize the likely lyrical insertions. What the clowns say likewise contains an occasional narrative embedding that deals with local gossip rather than with history. Still, the work evidently fits into a dramatic matrix since it opens with an exchange of declarations in the present tense that elicit response alternately from the spectators and the rain gods. Implicit in what the clowns say to each other is the world view which the Tewa *chimiky'ana'kowa* defines, although that remains an unsupported assumption since no specific reference I am able to recognize cites the creation story in the way that the Seneca creation narrative is explicitly invoked in the longhouse Thank-You Prayer, or the way in which a fundamentalist Protestant sermon might very well invoke a particular verse from Genesis 1 or 2, say. It is important to remember, though, that whether implicitly or explicitly a *chimiky'ana'kowa* is fundamental to virtually any sacred dramatic work and to many, if not most, *telapnaawe*.

Even in a simple translation like that of Laski's San Juan text as opposed to Hale's bilingual rendering of the Iroquois work, careful reading can help to determine how lyrical or colloquial a given work may be, and in deciding whether it is essentially a story or potentially a dramatic script. Doing so may also require a thoughtful consideration of any available context. Some texts, like those of both Laski and Hale, come complete with ethnographic descriptions and linguistic or lexical glosses. Others, like many of those Rothenberg includes, do not, although his endnotes and innovative front matter go far to stir a sharp awareness of the tribal, oral roots of the material he includes. A poet himself, he adds provocative interpretations of his own—sometimes highly subjective—and whether he is right or wrong in doing so, his enthusiasm for the material and its tribal origins at least stimulates readers to transcend the mindset that ordinary printed poetry invokes. Still other anthologies, meanwhile, like the earlier ones of Cronyn or Brandon, offer the reader less documentary support, and are best ignored, in my view, or read with great caution.

With a bit of reflection on the reader's part, a piece like Rothenberg's reworking of the aforementioned Eskimo caribou-hunting song can be called dramatic, just as others may seem evidently so without the help of documentation when gleaned alertly. "You, you caribou," it opens, in a statement obviously addressed by a hunter to the creature he is stalking (see p. 43; see also pp. 350–51). And given the way Rothenberg deploys his orthography in attempting to reconstruct cadence and pause, the work can also be called lyrical, or at least treated that way when read aloud. Conceivably, it could even be scored and sung, all the more effectively, perhaps, by someone who has read similar works compiled from Eskimo sources and who has explored ethnographic literature and perhaps even found a way to examine the music of arctic peoples. "Yes you," it continues,

> long legs
> yes you
> long ears
> you with the long neck hair—
> From far off you're little as a louse:
> Be my great swan, fly to me,
> big bull
> cari-bou-bou-bou.

Even if they do not duplicate the lyrical properties contained in the original Netsilik version syllable for syllable, tone for tone, or stress for stress, the graphics here serve to convey visually that a patterned voice is at work audibly, and they prompt a careful, open-minded reading of the poem that can re-create or at least imply vestiges of lyricism in what the speaker says to his other-than-human quarry in a world still soft enough for men and animals to commune.

Other printed lyrics can likewise fit the narrative mode, or so I would bid readers to speculate by looking carefully at texts and remaining mindful of how they originate or might have originated in a performance mode. Beginning in the past tense, this Inuit sample, included in *Shaking the Pumpkin*, tells of the earlier phase of the *inoote* when the world was soft enough for creatures to change shape back and forth (Rothenberg, p. 42):

> In the very earliest time,
> when both people and animals lived on earth,
> a person could become an animal if he wanted to
> and an animal could become a human being.
> Sometimes they were people
> and sometimes animals
> and there was no difference.
> All spoke the same language.
> That was the time when words were like magic.
> The human mind had mysterious powers.
> A word spoken by chance
> might have strange consequences.
> It would suddenly come alive
> and what people wanted to happen could happen—
> all you had to do was say it.
> Nobody could explain this:
> That's the way it was.

While this English rendering sounds fairly colloquial, I would move it toward the lyric side of the voice continuum since each line contains a somewhat parallel, solitary subject–predicate unit. Exceptions occur in the first line, where the isolated prepositional phrase designates the ancient time of the action; in the sixth line, where the missing subject offsets the otherwise strictly parallel structure of line five; and in lines eleven and twelve, which are each limited respectively to noun part and verb part of a single two-line independent clause, possibly to underscore the "strangeness" of the way language worked in that ancient time. That broad feature of relative syntactical uniformity gives the poem an internal rhythm commensurate with the patterned language of the lyrical voice in conventionally metered English verse.

I am dealing with a translation here, of course, and know nothing of the donor language and little about the culture beyond what its translated poems disclose. Consequently, I may be attributing to the work a quality of voice absent in the original. Hymes makes an observation that may apply in such a case. Patterns of deep poetry exist in good works, he suggests, and "make so many Indian narratives a kind of poetry." "Such patterns are acquired and employed without awareness," he adds. "They are not topics of analytic discussion," as Europe and America's printed poems have become. "The languages lack terms for them." Nonetheless, "for Indian and non-Indian alike, the patterning [can] be brought to awareness by the discovery of an appropriate method" (1987, p. 42). Given a reasonably literal translation, that method may include a search for semantic patterns that survive the linguistic trauma of removal to print. It may also permit a thoughtful reader at least to posit the voice of an original performance.

Since it contains no dramatic embeddings I also consider the above lyric a simple narrative, as opposed to what I call a complex narrative, which quotes statements made by one character to some other during the course of the action. Likewise, the Eskimo caribou-hunting song is a simple dramatic lyric since there are no interludes whatsoever wherein a speaker relates or refers to some event that occurred in the past. Accordingly, both the Iroquois Condolence Ritual and the San Juan Rain God Drama are both complex dramatic works because they contain narrative embeddings. Similarly, a narrative like the Zuni "Boy and the Deer," or "The Beginning," are complex matrices since they contain dramatic embeddings. Any matrix, whether narrative or dramatic or in the colloquial or lyrical voice, can be complex depending on whether it contains embeddings.

A narrative embedding can even contain a dramatic sub-embedding, in fact, inviting the reader to imagine how the story-teller would modify her voiced delivery. Or the reader might wish to do so in reading the work aloud. In such cases, it is good, too, to go so far as to imagine a storytelling venue. That is fairly easy for me to do because I have spent many hours in hogans, chapter houses, or local school buildings listening to Navajos perform. Readers who have not done so, however, can stimulate an active imagination by reading about performances. During the initial stage of my research the work of Dell Hymes helped me consider-ably, as did an early but still serviceable essay by Robert A. Georges, "Toward an Understanding of Storytelling Events." More recently, Claire Farrer has done an excellent job of describ-ing a ceremonial setting in *Living Life's Circle*, where she ac-counts for poetic activity in her description of the annual Mes-calero girls' puberty ceremony (Farrer, pp. 33–59). Likewise, a narrative episode might exist in a dramatic statement as the oppo-site kind of sub-embedding. That occurs in "The Boy and the Deer," in fact, when the boy first meets his human mother and reminds her, in a past-tense statement, "My Sun Father made you pregnant. When he made you pregnant you sat there and your belly began to grow large" (Tedlock: 1978, p. 25).

Obviously, such classifications involve judgements and can be challenged or disputed. I have found, however, that the ensuing discussions can be helpful, even where agreement cannot be reached, because they require a careful, analytical reexamination (I am tempted to say reconstruction) of the poem in question and of any supplementary material that may help readers gain a grasp of the work's cultural context. Hence, attempting to classify them requires reading individual texts actively and closely. It also re-quires accepting them as something more by far than "myths," "legends," "folktales," or artlessly fashioned statements by marginalized peoples with no preserved past or fully retained world view rivaling those present in Eastern or Western tradi-tions. Let me promptly add as well that such active reading can be very exciting indeed because it leads to strikingly different modes of thought and expression, some of which may address today's conditions in ways that mainstream European works do not.

By now it should be evident that some kind of structural paradigm might help to facilitate the careful examination of material
for its own aesthetic sake, and for the sake of understanding tribal
peoples not merely as hapless victims of a European juggernaut,
but as survivors able nonetheless to preserve their cultural wealth
verbally as well as materially. Looking at mute artifacts in museums actually says very little about the Native American past, at
least in poetry's resonating way of articulating ideas and perceptions. As a ready framework for a simple taxonomy, I suggest representing the voice continuum with a solid horizontal line ranging
from pure lyric at the left to fully colloquial at the right (or vice
versa; the mutual positions are interchangeable). Then I attempt
to locate a particular less-than-pure lyric, such as the Inuit word
song, a little on the lyrical side. A pure song, on the other hand,
belongs at the very end of the line, just as a flatly conversational
statement stands at the opposite end of the continuum. Then I
cross that solid horizontal line with a broken vertical one to signify the opposite modes of dramatic and narrative, which unlike
voice are not a matter of degree, but rather must be one or the
other.

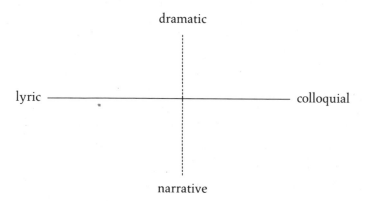

The San Juan Rain God Drama or the Iroquois Condolence Ritual would thus classify as a colloquial drama and a lyrical one,
respectively, while the Zuni "Boy and the Deer" and the Inuit

account of people and animals changing shape could be identified as a complex, fairly colloquial narrative and a simple, somewhat lyrical narrative, respectively. Hypothetically, all texts could be located somewhere in that scheme, allowing for a systematic way of approaching them, of comparing the corpus of one tribe's poetry with that of another, and permitting the systematic comparison and contrast as well of Native American texts with standard Anglo-European ones.

This scheme should be used carefully, however, at least when it comes to examining texts. Readers should be conscious of the medium of print and aware that the words and letters they see merely symbolize such linguistic components as phonemes or signifying units of sound, morphemes or significant units of meaning, and meaningful syntactical or grammatical elements—all originally spoken and written down only secondarily. By so doing, those readers can learn to listen within the mind's ear and activate the mind's eye with the cues provided by the text. What is written down can be internalized as the sound of the active human voice; what is seen at first as mere print can be transformed by an auditory imagination into something first heard and then richly envisioned as a reconstructed poetic event in its full cultural context. Doing so represents an effort in reintegrating the poetic process that originally occurs as an actual performance, but can disintegrate in the reductive process of writing it down, often in translation.

Let me offer one example of what I mean, which I draw from Margo Astrov's *The Winged Serpent* rather than from the primary written sources she used. I do so to underscore the point that readers can initially experience a sense of the performed poetry implicit in any such printed anthology if they approach the language with active thoughtfulness. Once they access such experiences, they can always refer to the primary source to learn more, not only about the text in its social setting, but about the culture which comprises that backdrop.

The Astrov volume contains seven Papago selections (pp. 192–202), including a war song, a woman's dream song, two death songs, a song from a sun ceremony, and three rain songs—all taken from Ruth Underhill's very fine volume, *Singing for Power*. The seventh selection consists of a three-page excerpt from *The Autobiography of a Papago Woman*—Underhill's published story of Maria Choma, which she arranged chronologically after listening through an interpreter. I will focus primarily on it. In its printed, translated form, it sounds colloquial and looks narrative, although it contains numerous dramatic embeddings. A question arises when dealing with autobiography, however: is it poetry, and if so, how? Answering may require spotting poetic properties in other material translated and transcribed from the same language community, or in spotting signs of poetic activity within the autobiographical text itself.

While the book has numerous imperfections (see Bataille, p. 89), this passage provides some guidelines in reaching a satisfactory conclusion. "On winter nights," Maria begins in the paragraph that opens Astrov's selection, "when we had finished our gruel or rabbit stew and lay back on our mats, my brothers would say to my father: 'My father, tell us something.'" And this second paragraph follows:

> My father would lie quietly upon his mat with my mother beside him and the baby between them. At last he would start slowly to tell us about how the world began. This is a story that can be told only in winter when there are no snakes about, for if the snakes heard they would crawl in and bite you. But in winter when the snakes are asleep, we tell these things. Our story about the world is full of songs, and when the neighbors heard my father singing they would open our door and step in over the high threshold. Family by family they came, and we made a big fire and kept the door shut against the cold night. When my father finished a sentence we would all say the last word after him. If anyone went to sleep he would stop. He would not speak any more. But we did not go to sleep. . . .

Notice the stated relationship here between singing and telling, along with the allusion to the father's power as a singer, which draws his neighbors. Notice, too, how in paragraph three she associates his songs with visions:

My father was a song maker, and he had visions even if he was not a medicine man. He always made a song for the big harvest festival, the one that keeps the world going right and that only comes every four years.

Armed with such visions and the ongoing balance which prevails in the world as their result, she explains in the next paragraph how her family joins others at "the Place of the Burnt Seeds," where "we camped together, many, many families, and we made images of the beautiful things that make life good for the desert people, like clouds and corn and squash and deer."

Her father, she goes on to say, once made such "an image of a mountain out of cactus ribs covered with white cloth. He had dreamed about this mountain and this is the song he made:

> There is a white shell mountain in the ocean
> Rising half out of the water.
> Green scum floats on the water.
> And the mountain turns around.

To Western ears, the connotation of the word *scum* is unfortunate and possibly misleading, but at least it forces us to envision the all-important water in the arid landscape whose needed rainfall dominates Papago religious practice. And it is important to realize that the lyrical dramatic embedding evokes the *visual image*—i.e., the vision her father makes with his song. It is important, too, to see the connection between the notion of "tell" in paragraph one, "singing" in paragraph two, "song-making" and "visions" in paragraph three, and "image-making" in paragraph four. In today's electronic reality, where poetry is reduced to a subcategory of literature, while song is conventionally associated principally with recordings—whether on videotape or compact discs—visual images are prepackaged outside the actively imaginative, envisioning domain of the viewer/listener instead of within the kind of visualizing imagination that reading requires; it is difficult to appreciate the integrative process of telling ◆ singing ◆ envisioning ◆ image-making, all facilitated by the words of a performing poet in an oral setting such as the one that Astrov's Papago woman describes.

A good poem unites those four components, however, in what becomes a single mental process, not a fragmentation wherein they are kept separate because fabricated externally as separate processes. A good reader, meanwhile, struggles to reunite them by (a) listening to the poem's voice, (b) paying attention to the mode (i.e., identifying the matrix and spotting its embeddings) and (c) applying the imagination to reconstruct the images that accompany a vision. Such holistic aural–visual production can result from the narrative that Astrov repeats in this particular selection, conveying an awareness of another culture's other world whose meaning to its inhabitants gets transmitted to the reader. That deep poetic quality which resides in what Underhill's narrator tells her rises to the text's surface in the clarity of its English. That quality resonates when read aloud with a colloquial rhythm commensurate with its thematic rhythm. Storytelling and singing thereby merge, and when brought together merge again as one with rainmaking and cycles of growing and harvesting.

Such an active reading of an anthologized selection may be enhanced by consulting the original source and then following that up with further investigation. Conceivably, that follow-up might ultimately include visiting a community or a site; examining its other arts and comparing visual designs with verbal elements of design; learning more about the tribe in question including its past, its world view, and as much of its ceremonial life as respectful inquiry allows; getting to know some of its people, perhaps eventually as a friend and a participant rather than an investigator; and discovering overall that whether material or verbal, that tribe's artifacts do not mere commodities to be priced or stored in museums, but projections of a living culture requiring the same kind of respectful involvement that any community's artifacts do when applied in everyday living or for special occasions. When a Navajo medicine man tells how he obtained the eagle feathers which adorn it, a prayerstick becomes an accessory to a powerful story that amplifies the ceremony which requires its use. As a weaver sings, she invests her work with her mother's voice as well as her own, or with that of her grandmother or whoever relayed it to her from an ancient source. A rug thus virtually sings with an underlying lyric that matches its graphic design.

I do not mean to trivialize or objectify the process of broadening the silence of print through direct experience. The difference is roughly like that between reading the libretto of *The Marriage of Figaro* without ever hearing an opera and actually attending a performance. Or it is like reading an album's lyrics as opposed to hearing the singer in concert. Such a full encounter is likely to alter your life in ways that poetry and other art ultimately instigate: not an inconceivable achievement given art's ultimate power. That is especially true of poetry, I believe; for with its special power of articulation it can either transform us to another venue in the manner of a storyteller or set another one dramatically before us, sometimes making this whole world a stage, sometimes staging some other world before our eyes. Beyond that, it can encourage readers literally to explore other cultures and other worlds with a new awareness contrary to hackneyed old assumptions about noble savages or hostile ones.

I urge caution in pursuing the voice-mode paradigm, however; abstract, theoretical constructs tend to acquire a life of their own that can overwhelm the particulars they treat. It is not my intent to create a scheme that subordinates its parts to the whole; rather, I seek a paradigm that relates individual texts to one another according to how they might sound in performance and how they alter the reality they take the measure of. I also seek a model that neither elevates nor subordinates Native American texts to Western ones or vice versa. Readers may favor one group of texts to another. Some may prefer to dismiss works taken from the so called canon in favor of texts from other cultures. Some may wish to emphasize the political implications of texts or advocate replacing one set of texts with another in a particular curriculum. All of that ultimately is a matter of taste, political preference, or judgement.

For my part, though, I wish to build a system that promises initial simplicity in formulating distinctions and permits comparison and contrast as objectively as possible. Since Native American poetry represents a newly discovered discourse, it may at first seem too exotic to treat systematically. Or in the current enthusiasm for things multicultural, it can be virtually dismissed as the work of marginalized people by demands for its inclusion in a curriculum with no understanding of its varied traditions or awareness of the implications of orality for print technology. Certainly it should be included, but not as the work of victims. Instead, it should be given its proper place in the pantheon of the world's noteworthy poetic expression in a systematic model that helps in understanding what poetry is, why it is important to a given culture and in the wider human community, and how it functions as sacred expression even where conventional Judeo-Christian thought or secular resistance to it might eclipse such a likelihood.

I like to suggest that readers of all poetry—whether lyric or colloquial, dramatic or narrative—should specify how they imagine they can "hear" its language and then explain why they think so. What are the measured qualities of the singing voice? Where in the spoken voice do they see the internal rhythm, and what looser patterns do they see in the so-called prose that would give it poetic dimensions when recited verbally? Is there thematic rhythm that resonates in partial repetition or topical reiteration? Likewise, I advise them to specify whether a given work belongs in a dramatic or a narrative matrix. Do we overhear someone speaking to someone else now in a world whose presence we have joined, or is a storyteller dispatching us to some other venue remote in time and place?

I recommend that they spot the dramatic embeddings of a narrative poem and the narrative embeddings in a dramatic matrix. That can be done while listening to the song lyrics prevalent in today's popular culture—arguably promoting a poetic renaissance featuring the lyric voice transmitted electronically. Film and video likewise have created an electronically transmitted venue for dramatic poetry and narrative alike in some interesting combinations. Sometimes those new electronic forms can best be appraised in the context of North America's still untapped, largely unrecognized traditions of tribal orality, which may ultimately serve as a better index of how poetry is applied in present-day culture than conventional literature allows.

In the process of establishing standards of appraisal and appreciation different from those which print allows in its conventional isolation from the performing voice, readers, listeners, and viewers might very well recognize new conceptions of the sacred along with new connections between Native American material, conventionally print-oriented poetic artifacts familiar through schooling, and the growing wellspring of poetry distributed by way of sound recordings, video, film, and even computer software. In many cases, Native American material may relate to films and video performances in ways yet unrecognized. Traditionally, poetry has played a part in Native American life in spite of its existence off the page. Off-page poetry may very well play a greater part in our own lives as well, or it may only appear to. All of that remains to be explored, and such exploration might very well begin by using the voice-mode paradigm as it emerges through the study in print of orally based North American tribal poetry.

In addition to exploring the books and journals that are now beginning to promote tribal poetry, readers can begin to explore the amazingly rich source material available through the Bureau of American Ethnology. For nearly a century and a half, that agency has been compiling invaluable bulletins and reports that include great quantities of material, albeit recognized as data rather than as poetry. A veritable Loeb Library presenting nothing less than a North American classical past, those volumes contain enormous quantities of poetic work, buttressed by rich cultural commentary. Virtually all of them beg for closer inspection as a vast wellspring of hitherto undiscovered poetry.

I speculate that once readers learn to recognize whether a particular selection is lyrical or colloquial; once they determine if it is dramatic or narrative and whether a dramatic work is multivoiced or univocal; and once they can decide if the speaker or speakers address other mortals or nonmortal beings, that work's deep poetic appeal can overcome, at least in part, the distorting effects of transcription and translation, especially when it is graphically reworked in the way that Rothenberg reworks some of the selections in *Shaking the Pumpkin*.

Once the words are connected with a specific speaker, however—such as a storyteller whose own voice prevails throughout the work or through whose voice various characters carry on dialog, or such as the hunter's dramatic voice in the Eskimo caribou song—readers can put the poem into a fixed locus relative to other poems. And once they recognize that the Zuni Ahayuuta twins seek to bond with humans just as someone like the hunter is verbalizing a sense of kinship with his prey, they can grasp the nature of human relationships with a greater-than-human reality. When monitored carefully, print can serve as a record of voices that have managed to survive drastic change and destructive incursions and still have something to tell us. Its North American tribal legacy has as much to offer as the so-called Old World's classical tradition or biblical past.

To take full measure of that potentially rich offering, however, we need to recognize something easy to overlook in an age when overamplified sound and oversized screen images have made careful reading an esoteric activity for arcane specialists and have overwhelmed the thoughtful reflection that literature invites. Poetry has become a brutally underesteemed art form. The term itself and how it has come to be used have contributed to that neglect. But to neglect poetry is to neglect what verbalizes the deepest, most essential condition of being human.

It has done alphabetical poetry no good to have fallen almost exclusively into the hands of academicians, especially given the current academic practice of placing one's own publishing career above the needs of students—or worse still, above the needs of nonacademic audiences. That situation is exacerbated by politicizing the curriculum in today's colleges—by the creation of a canon as straw man to be demolished for the sake of reconstructing the past or of revising it to suit a specific ideology, whether on the proverbialized left or right. It is worsened further still by polarizing poetry according to race, class, gender, or cultural origin. A given poetic work may be fitted by any such label; but when conjoined with other poetry from the same or other sources it plays its part in projecting a greater-than-human reality for people who otherwise remain merely human and who persist in struggling to grasp what that means.

GLOSSARY

ALPHABETICAL POETRY (pp. 7,10). Poetry that is composed in manuscript form and whose spoken dimension exists only secondarily. It remains an open question to me whether a poem erstwhile harvested from an oral performance, put into print, and in that written form outlives or outdistances whoever may have once recited it for an audience of listeners is alphabetical. Should we consider Homer's *Iliad* or *Odyssey* alphabetical poetry, for example? What are the circumstances that make it literature rather than oral poetry? The detailed particulars of the differences between alphabetical and oral poetry remain to be fixed or even fully appreciated.

CHIMIKY'ANA'KOWA (pp. 98, 100). One of two different kinds of narrative recognized by the Zunis in a distinction potentially useful to mainstream critics, scholars, and general readers. Both types belong to that temporally distant world, the *inoote* or the long-ago (q.v.). Regarded as literally true, it belongs to a period when the world was soft and easily shaped and reshaped. The events it tells account for the way things are. The opening chapters of Genesis is the standard *chimiky'ana'kowa* throughout the so-called Western World. Every culture has a *chimiky'-ana'kowa*, which influences its traditional poetry heavily and even reaches into its secular poetic works. See also *Telapnaawe*.

COLLOQUIAL VOICE (pp. 39, 40, 64). Less tightly patterned than lyrical voice, colloquial poetry is the product of the natural speaking voice. When transmitted in printed form it is likely to exist as prose. It becomes more the voice of conversation, at least in its pure form, although like lyrical poetry it occurs as a matter of degree. It may be flatly conversational, or it may exhibit some lyrical properties.

COMPLEX NARRATIVE (p. 114). A narrative containing one or more dramatic embeddings is complex. It quotes statements made by one character to some other during the course of the action. *See also* simple narrative.

CREATION NARRATIVES (p. 3). Along with the complex of poetic works they engender, these narratives are fundamental to what emerges in a poetic tradition of a people and its greater-than-human belief system. They often verbalize what lies at the heart of all that emerges as that people's culture. In a secular age such as the one we currently live in, creation narratives are apt to be overlooked as an important source of literature. That is a major oversight, especially if academic critics are serious about taking full measure of nonwestern or tribal poetic traditions. See also *Chimiky'ana'kowa*.

DESIGN (p. 7). When spoken of here, design presupposes some inner conception of order that somehow finds manifest expression on the surface of a poetic work, no matter what the medium.

DRAMATIC MODE (p. 81). As opposed to the narrative mode, which involves the voice of a narrator repeating a story in the past tense, the dramatic mode usually involves more than one voice appealing to a third party speaking in the present tense in anticipation of an immediate response while an audience overhears or looks on. Elements of the narrative mode can be embedded in a dramatic work, just as a narrative might contain dramatic elements.

DRAMATIC PRESENT (p. 82). Because everything in a dramatic work occurs in a staged immediacy, any distinction marking past or future in the dramatic mode collapses into a dramatic present. To secure that present, spectators and participants alike gather in a world apart—down a kiva ladder, inside a longhouse or a ceremonial hogan. To watch our own dramatic productions we in mainstream Euro-American culture generally walk under a marquis, pass through a lobby, and present a ticket to an usher at an inner doorway to the separate immediacy of a darkened hall that we call a theater.

ELECTRONIC POETRY (pp. 8, 10). A subset of poetry transmitted by way of film or audio and videotape, or composed digitally and distributed via computer technology. Electronic poetry more often than not gives the illusion of being recited spontaneously, although it usually comes from a written script and hence may qualify as literature in the strict, letter-oriented sense of the term, at least in some instances. Such distinctions need to be made.

EMBEDDING (pp. 87, 83–85). A dramatic passage inserted into a narrative matrix, or vice versa, which thus renders a matrix complex rather than simple. If Shakespeare's *Hamlet* is a dramatic matrix overall, lines 59 through 80 in Act I, scene v is a narrative embedding within it, for in that passage the Ghost tells the prince how he had been murdered in his sleep by Claudius, thereby becoming a storyteller. Such a narrative passage can be embedded anywhere within a dramatic matrix, just as in a narrative any character can speak to another, thus producing a dramatic embedding in a narrative matrix.

INOOTE (pp. 97, 99–101). A Zuni term used to designate a world elsewhere in time and place where sacred stories occurred. It is a world belonging to the long-ago, before this world hardened so that change would be retarded. Communication took place between all beings, human or otherwise. It is a time of beginnings, where the softer, long-ago cosmos is not yet fully formed. See also *chimiky'ana'kowa, telapnaawe.*

LITERATURE (p. 6). Employed rather loosely to include a number of similarly broad "genres" of written discourse, this term conventionally specifies poetry, fiction, and drama more by assumption than by deliberate designation. It exists by and large in close association with print. The term now has limitations because it presupposes existence on the printed page and hence precludes thoughtful reference to orally composed and transmitted poetry, whether in live performance or stored electronically.

LYRIC (pp. 37, 38, 45, 64). A property of what I call voice. Poetry associated with the singing voice can be considered lyric. Its properties may include such qualities as stress and rhythm described in conventional textbooks, or it may be described in terms of the finely stylized voice of pure song. In its extreme form it exists as steadily cadenced discourse that can be represented by musical notation or as printed verse. *See also* Colloquial.

MATRIX (pp. 82, 87, 88). A term borrowed from mathematics that designates an ordered array of individual units belonging to a set. As used here it can be defined as a given work's overriding shell extending from the opening word to the last. It functions to distinguish mode, whether narrative or dramatic, and to allow the further recognition of embeddings within a particular work, whether a dramatic embedding in a narrative matrix or a narrative embedding in a dramatic matrix. Thereby refined distinctions of structure may be made with reference to the mode of a particular work.

MODE (pp. 81, 108). This is a term I use to differentiate between dramatic and narrative forms of poetry. Unlike voice, which can be lyrical or colloquial to a matter of degree, mode occurs in an absolute state as either narrative or dramatic. Hence it appeals to form or structure, whether that of the storyteller repeating chronologically something having occurred in the past in a direct appeal to an audience, or that of a person addressing a third party in an immediate exchange isolated from any sense of past or future as an audience listens or looks on in an existential present. *See also* Dramatic Mode, Narrative Mode.

NARRATIVE MODE (pp. 81, 87). The narrative mode exists when audiences listen to a lone speaker addressing no one in particular telling exclusively of prior events that occurred someplace apart and remote from where the audience now sits. If an audience leaves its everyday world to attend or witness a dramatic work, a storyteller brings another world from some real or imagined time and place in the past into this world—at least speculatively. A narrative poem ultimately comes from the voice of a single storyteller directly addressing a specific audience without expecting it to issue a particular reply. Dramatic units can be embedded in a narrative work, just as the narrative components may exist in a dramatic matrix.

NARRATIVE PAST (p. 97). The chief distinction of a narrative matrix from its dramatic counterpart—at least in Native American storytelling—is its removal to a far-off and often sacred past. Whereas the action in drama is immediate because it summons elements of the sacred from a time and place elsewhere into the arena of the dramatic present, narrative transports an audience to a world elsewhere in time and place alike. That other world can be referred to as the *narrative past*.

ORAL POETRY (pp. 6–7). A species of the broad genus poetry distinguished as that which is fundamentally transmitted by the human voice and monitored by ear. Only secondarily is it recorded and distributed through the medium of print and, more recently, through electronic media. *See also* Alphabetical Poetry.

POESIS (p. 19). An awareness—recovered by way of careful observation and expressed systematically—of how a given narrative or dramatic work is created, stored, and maintained whether orally, alphabetically, or electronically, together with a commensurate awareness of its poetic qualities, both deeply and on its textured surface.

POETRY (pp. 6, 7). Herein used not in reference to a literary genre, but rather more broadly in replacement of the term *literature*, which may have outlived its usefulness. Defined here as that art form whose primary medium is language whether written or spoken (or sung); whether recorded in print, on video, or audio tape; or whether packaged in the human memory according to various mnemonic techniques. It is an art form as readily oral as written, and hence not to be confined to the conventional page. *See also* Alphabetical Poetry, Deep Poetry, Oral Poetry, Recited Poetry, Surface Poetry, Written Poetry.

PRINTED POETRY (pp. 8–10). Conventionally positioned in books and periodicals, printed poetry is marked by a certain intentionality that can be applied more deliberately than oral poetry might apply it. Working slowly and carefully, an "author" thus "writes" a novel or "composes" a poem in solitude or isolation, using a pen or word-processor or some other instrument that applies graphic units, instead of producing vocally made sounds extemporaneously for people who have come to listen to him. As a term it is virtually interchangeable with written or alphabetical poetry.

PROSE (pp. 11, 65). As opposed to verse or what is commonly (and carelessly) called poetry, prose is a form of alphabetical poetry which more resembles vernacular speech. Thus it can be arranged more loosely on the printed page margin to margin instead of being carefully assembled line by line. When the lyric poetry of a nonliterate people is carelessly translated and transcribed as prose rather than in some carefully assembled poetic style, the result can tend to mute the artistry present in the original poetic performance.

RECITED POETRY (p. 9). Virtually the same as oral poetry, it exists by way of the active human voice monitored live by audiences who listen, usually watch, and respond in some interactive way that may range from silence to applause to some sort of verbalized response.

SACRED (pp. 12–14). No easy term to explain, especially in a capsule summary, the sacred applies to poetry to a degree not properly recognized in a world increasingly secularized, or seemingly so. Nonetheless, I maintain throughout this volume that poetry rests on deep spiritual underpinnings that crave expression throughout the human community. Once it is recognized that the sacred is not necessarily limited to any particular religious doctrine or complex of belief systems like those founded on the Old Testament, poetry can be accepted as a widespread effort to connect the inner self and the natural with what dwells outside the self and beyond nature. Thus I recognize the sacred as any expressed apprehension of what Karl Luckert terms "a greater-than-human-reality" in his attempt to define religion (1976, p. 5).

SACRED TEXTS (p. 22). More plentiful than readers, critics, and scholars generally acknowledge in secularized Western culture, sacred texts range widely from the "self-evident truths" cited in the Declaration of Independence to Jonathan Swift's "Sweetness and Light," or Matthew Arnold's "best that has been thought and said"; or from Kant's Categorical Imperative to Thomas Carlyle's vision of history as "the first distinct product of man's spiritual nature" and "his earliest expression of what can be called Thought" (p. 80) to Ralph Waldo Emerson's Oversoul. Sacred texts exist abundantly as well in the various facets of mass and popular culture, ranging from songs and tv commercials to films and video productions, in an ongoing effort to verbalize a "greater-than-human-reality."

SIMPLE NARRATIVE (p. 114). A narrative is simple when it contains no dramatic embeddings. *See also* Complex Narrative.

STRUCTURALISM (p. 4). Views all social and cultural phenomena including literary texts as disparate units of signifying structure. It "undertakes to explain how the phenomena have achieved their significance . . . by reference to an underlying system" that can be seen and described objectively as a fixed set "of rules and codes" (Abrams, pp. 280–281).

TEXT (pp. 11–12). This term has generally referred to printed poetry or what has conventionally been called literature. It very well could be widened to refer to the way poetry is stored in any medium. We could thus conceivably speak of a written text; or recorded texts whether audio or video; of a cinematext in the case of film; or even of a ceremonial text, which recognizes the human memory as a legitimate way of preserving performed poetry.

TELAPNAAWE (pp. 98, 101). Like its counterpart, the *chimiky'ana'kowa* in the Zuni dichotomy that recognizes two basic kinds of sacred narrative, the *telapnaawe* is set in the long ago while the world was still soft. Unlike the former, however, it takes place slightly later in a world that has hardened some. And it is considered more a fiction—a story whose truth can be questioned or is not necessarily to be accepted literally but has a lesson to teach. The Zuni dichotomy may be useful in establishing meaningful distinctions among mainstream Western narratives, such as the Bible or the Hesiodic-Homeric poetic legacy. See also *chimiky'ana'kowa, inoote.*

THEMATIC RHYTHM (pp. 59, 67, 70). Not necessarily the surface rhythm nor the overtly repeated pattern of syntax and sound clearly manifest in lyrical poetry, thematic rhythm exists in poetry in the form of conceptual patterns rather than patterns of sound made manifest by meter or rhyme. Thus whether colloquial or lyrical, a poetic work can acquire thematic rhythm from reiterated thematic units, units of slightly varying syntax which repeat a motif or an idea, or from patterns of thought that may be expressed colloquially as well as lyrically.

VERSE (p. 11). What is conventionally called poetry might better be called verse—at least when printed poetry is referred to. Because the formal patterns of verse are generally more rigidly established, when stored in print it is carefully arrayed on the page with wide, uneven right-hand margins, in contrast with *prose.*

VOICE (pp. 34, 76). The primary medium of poetry absent the mediation of print. Voice is the absolute sound of poetry whether spoken or sung. It reacquires its natural purity when a written work is read aloud or performed, as with the stage production of a play or when a vocalist performs in front of an audience. At its extremes, it may exist colloquially or lyrically, projected respectively by the speaking or the singing voice. Ranging from one to the other, it exists as a matter of degree in a given performance. *See also* Colloquial, Lyric.

WRITTEN POETRY (p. 7). May be differentiated according to whether it is originally composed in manuscript form whose spoken dimensions exist as it were secondarily, at least until it is read aloud and performed. It assumes its full distinction from oral poetry, however, by virtue of being composed alphabetically apart from any audience gathered to listen as it materializes vocally. *See also* Alphabetical Poetry, Printed Poetry.

NOTES

Chapter One

1. Paul Zumthor—an exceptional scholarly source because he sidesteps mainstream European and European-American literary or theoretical models in his examination of oral poetry worldwide—provides a starting point for developing an aesthetic by securing a way to distinguish between oral and written poetry (p. 22). All poetry, he suggests, represents five phases of existence, "so to speak." They include (1) production, (2) transmission, (3) reception, (4) storage, and (5) repetition. Oral performance, he goes on to say, "embraces 2 and 3 and in cases of improvisation, 1, 2 and 3."

2. Walter Ong explores the distinctions I am trying to make here more elaborately and on somewhat different terms. I urge anyone interested in pursuing them to consult him. I also recommend consulting Havelock (1963, 1976). See Laski, especially p. 37, where recited narrative is used to train the young actors preparing to participate in the upcoming rain god ceremony.

3. See Miller, p. 12, however, for a somewhat more normative application of the term *text*: "By 'text' is meant a single example or document, a version or a single telling of a tale, better or worse than an ideal. While controversial, observation of living traditions does indicate that a native community will have an ideal version of a text, a definitive telling by an acclaimed teller that implies the standard for the group." During the years I spent composing this volume and assembling it for publication, attention to writing, print technology, and printed texts has been rapidly growing. I cannot pretend to have kept up with that scholarship; indeed scholarly production accelerates almost with the velocity of a body falling through space, it seems, and it is sometimes frustratingly unrealistic to try to keep up in any field. Several very recent works, however, can help direct the interested reader to some of the fascinating material now available in print and printed texts, both in a broad historical context and in the contemporary context of the cyber-electronic transmission of language. See, for example, Martin; Levenston; and Kaufmann, especially his introduction on "Print and the Novel" (pp. 13–35). For a fundamental grasp of the place of print in the modern world, I especially recommend Eisenstein's monumental work.

4. I discuss the *inoote* in Chapter Four. But in mentioning this distinction here, I also think of Giambattista Vico and of what Northrop Frye does with Vico's distinctions, which leads to fruitful considerations of myths and other

narratives, including not only so-called folktales, legends, and parables, but to documented historical narratives as well. See Frye, chapters 1 and 2, especially pp. 32–35.

Chapter Two

1. Various English versions exist, widely mixed in quality and comprehensiveness. The best are found in Hewitt (1903) and Parker (1923), while Tooker (1979, pp. 31–68) provides a readable modification and Bierhorst (1985, pp. 194–200) summarizes it well, adds good basic documentation, and reflects, however briefly, an uncommonly receptive awareness of the poetic style that accompanies its presentation in an oral setting.

2. While I have located other written accounts (e.g., Chafe, pp. 17–45, repr. in Tooker: 1979, pp. 58–68; Foster, pp. 286–403), and while they exhibit the variation that multiple translations usually display, I like best the Richard Johnny John version that Jerome Rothenberg harvested for publication in *Shaking the Pumpkin* (pp. 4–9).

3. Variants exist (see Wallace: 1986, p. vii, for a guide to extant English translations), but A. C. Parker's adaptation from the Seth Newhouse version represents the most comprehensive printed English version that I know of, and it is perhaps the best as well. That text combines the legend of how warfare ended among the tribes with the expository description of the terms of peace that united them in an enduring confederacy. In a useful introduction to their retelling of Newhouse's English rendering (pp. 183–92), Sandars and Peek justifiably call the narrative portion an epic. There are indeed enough elements of the heroic in Dekanawida's origins and exploits to warrant the use of the term *epic*, and a certain poetic tone emerges from the account even though Newhouse may not have created it as deliberately as Richard Johnny John creates textured poetry in his translation of the Thank-You Prayer. Meanwhile, hints of the poetic also appear in the English translation of the expository portion of the text, which describes the conditions of the treaty whose origins the narrative segment traces.

4. Better poetry exists in that text than in any other recovered so far from existing translations of the *Constitution*. Bierhorst's English version, which he reconstructs from Hale and Hewitt (Bierhorst: 1974, see p. 119), is especially poetic. Verbalized in an idiom that appears to reflect the poetic power of Iroquois oratory, it also displays the same kind of careful structure evident in the Thank-You Prayer.

Chapter Three

1. A few of today's contemporaries in the growing field of ethnopoetics have explored the relationship between poetry and song, most notably Hymes (1981), Rothenberg, Sherzer and Woodbury, and Tedlock (1978). David McAlister, too, deserves a special place in that group, although he fixes more of an ethnomusicologist's gaze on the material he considers. Among a handful of others I know of who attempt to close the gap between poetry and music by highlighting the dynamics of voice in the production of lyrics, I single out William Powers,

who elevates the use of vocables in Lakota song to poetic activity, and David Leeson Shaul, who examines Hopi poetry in a musical context and hence initiates a careful consideration of voice as a poetic property. None of these writers claims the title of literary critic, however, and the academic literary establishment continues to overlook a relationship important in recognizing how poetry transcends the narrow boundaries of the silent page. In *Ethnocriticism,* for example, Arnold Krupat's otherwise admirable effort to overcome conventional barriers, the place of music in poetic performance is all but ignored.

2. What makes poetry poetic is not just the more closely fixed patterns of meter and rhyme or other smaller units of sound that combine to achieve texture at the work's surface. Additional properties make it poetic and they range widely. They may include such elements as tropes or figures of speech, configurations of theme or structure or plot, and even seemingly irregular configurations of sound. I make no attempt to provide anything like a complete list here. That task, too, remains for others to consider.

3. Whenever English versions of Native American poetic works were attempted during the earlier nineteenth century, the practice of employing the then-established conventions of English lyric poetry was apparently common, even among Native American translators themselves. George Copway, for example, was an Objibwe who converted to Christianity and went on to produce "one of the first histories of an Indian nation written in English by an Indian" (Chapman, p. 30). Interspersed throughout that work are his English renditions of songs together with transliterations (see, for example, Copway, pp. 106, 128, 163). Interestingly, the translations are cast in the traditional ballad stanza form, reinforcing the impression that Ojibwe lyrics have a balladlike sound about them in that language. Coupled with Schoolcraft's translations and with highly popular works like Longfellow's *Song of Hiawatha*, such passages reinforced the idea that Native American poetry and song exhibit very much the same traits common to English and American verse. Nor are current liberally reconstructed free-verse reworkings—sometimes called interpretations—necessarily any less misleading. In an effort to pull away from the highly metrical conventions of the nineteenth century, for example, in *The Magic Word*, William Brandon creates the impression that Native American lyrics display the same highly impressionistic, personally reflected quality associated with today's unstructured free verse. That is a hazardous assumption to promote.

4. The term *incremental repetition* originates with Gummere (pp. 194, 252–56), and is used by Barnes (1922) in her discussion of the stylistics of Native American poetry, still a useful work.

5. At the 1992 annual Navajo Studies Conference in Window Rock, Arizona, Mr. Bahe Billy, a Navajo singer, performed a number of songs he had composed. Musically they were fully Navajo—traditional in tone and tempo—although the lyrics were in English. Mr. Billy presented them with characteristic Navajo humor, which was intensified by the juxtaposition of conventional Navajo melodics and English words. This was straight-out lyric poetry at its purest, and it anticipates something that I expect to see more and more of from the adaptive Nava-

jos. As I listened to him, I kept thinking that the only way to do his poetry justice in print would be to follow Natalie Curtis's lead and include a score with the lyrics, which might very well be arrayed on the page with some of the graphic features that Rothenberg, Swann, (1985) or Tedlock (1978) develop.

6. Vera Laski first recorded the San Juan Rain God Drama in a curtailed form sometime during the forties; she was permitted to do so only because it was feared for a while, that after the war there would no longer be enough men left to perform it again. That version was published by the American Folklore Society in 1958 and is no longer in print. Jerome Rothenberg "adapted the verses [and] reworked the dialogue" to include it in his *Shaking the Pumpkin*, which Doubleday published in 1972. In his own words, he altered Laski's original text slightly to create "a mock clown-style in English" (p. 439). His anthology went out of print, meanwhile, and was reissued by the University of New Mexico Press, but without the Rain God Drama. I am not sure I know why, but I have been told that some people at San Juan Pueblo were displeased to learn that Laski had produced a text in the first place. When I learned about those objections, I consulted with an elder from San Juan to seek his advice on sharing either of the two printed English versions with my students. He replied that since Laski did not record material considered essentially sacred, in his estimation no harm would result.

7. A major question arises regarding earlier, less carefully assembled English versions of Native American poetic material. Can deep poetry be recognized in all printed translations, no matter how badly investigators failed to observe it in the donor language or overlooked possibilities such as those that Tedlock or Hymes explore? Although it needs to be addressed, that issue cannot be easily resolved, especially at the present time. Under such rubrics as deconstructionism and postmodernism, major assumptions about analytic techniques and the enduring value of literary artistry have been severely challenged of late in a preoccupation with power and empowerment. Likewise, debates accompanying a rising postcolonial awareness tend to pit alternative cultures against those of hitherto dominant Western imperialism in an adversarial framework. A mood of political vindictiveness overshadows the aesthetic nuances of finer poetic considerations in the present intellectual and cultural climate. In brief, it has become easier and more fashionable right now to subordinate an inquiring, apolitical search for qualities like thematic rhythm or properties of the lyric voice to a general denunciation of colonialism and racist hegemony. In his foreword to Anne Smith's recently published volume of Ute narratives originally compiled in the late thirties, Joseph G. Jorgensen offers a good, if partisan, summary of how postmodernist thinking has overshadowed efforts in the empirical analysis of texts harvested by members of the dominant culture from Native Americans (pp. xxvii–xxviii, nn. 18 and 19).

Smith's volume of Ute narratives, incidentally, provides a good test case for determining whether deep poetry can survive efforts to assemble texts from Native American sources without regard for poetic worth. She seeks cultural nuances rather than poetic ones. Rather than locating it according to more purely aesthetic terms, her notion of style is bounded more by the social scientist's consideration of such features as "the absence of pattern numbers, the frequent use of anal and sexual references, the small amount of cultural detail; the general light and humorous tone of the tales," etc. (Smith, p. 257). As for the narratives themselves, they appear to require a very careful look.

Chapter Four

1. This is a place where it might seem appropriate to make a direct reference to current literary theory so abundant as I assemble this material in the early 1990s. I am tempted, for example, to try to apply M. M. Bakhtin's terms *monologic* and *dialogic,* which could conceivably be used in an effort to refine the broad distinction I wish to forge between a univocal narrative and the multiple voices that conventionally make up a dramatic work. Similarly, I might easily be tempted to draw vocabulary and related concepts from other theories currently being used, especially in academic settings. I have chosen to avoid such terms and approaches, however, and I do so for two reasons, using Bakhtin as a case in point with both. First, I do not believe that terms like his apply to traditional Native American poetry, since Bakhtin relies exclusively on printed texts without demonstrating that he considered their preliterate origins. Nor did he appear to listen to narrative or dramatic poetry performed in tribal settings. In comparing the epic with the novel, for example, he perceived the former exclusively through the lithic medium of print, which cannot possibly duplicate the elasticity of any sort of orally transmitted narrative—an elasticity that still prevails on the Navajo reservation. The epic, writes Bakhtin, "has come down to us [as] an absolutely completed and finished generic form, whose constitutive feature is the transferral of the world it describes to an absolute past of national beginnings and peak times." It "is impossible to change," the "tradition of the past is sacred," and the texts it yields provide "no consciousness of the possible relativity of any past" (p. 15). That may be the case with Europe's Homeric epics, with *Chanson de Roland,* or with *Beowulf,* which exist only as printed fossilized versions of once-dynamic oral traditions. But the sacred stories of the Navajos or the Zunis which speak of tribal "beginnings and peak times" do indeed change with each telling to this day. In describing what the Zunis call the *inoote* or the time long ago when the world was soft, traditional storytellers are constantly playing that world off against this one in what becomes a living tradition that remains forever relevant and relative to life today.

Second, as much as possible I wish to avoid applying theoretical models that emanate from non-Native sources or that impose norms either implicitly or explicitly whose sources are foreign to practitioners of tribal poetic discourse. Systems or standards drawn from sources originating with literate European traditions should be applied to Native poetic artifacts only with circumspect caution. I myself prefer merely to make frequent comparisons between poetic practices that emerge from Native American traditions and practices arising out of print cultures like those of the so-called Old World. And I do so without regard to political and economic domination. Should readers so wish, I encourage them to apply theoretical models to Native American poetic works themselves, or to use such works to test theories and hypotheses that come out of Europe. I do not see that as my own task here, however, where I am simply trying to introduce Native American texts as simply yet as systematically as possible. Above all, I do not wish to apply any of the theories that seem to pass in and out of fashion so swiftly during these poststructuralist, postmodern times of collision between electronic media and print media, between economic systems, or between clashing views of culture.

2. Let me quote Tedlock (1987, p. 332) for some help in making this point, since his views most nearly match mine and since he capably places his observations beyond the restrictive postures of current literary theorists, few indeed of whom turn at all to nonliterate sources for their primary observations. In cultures like those of the Zuni or the Navajo, where oral traditions survive vibrantly, Tedlock suggests that "a narrator, instead of describing a war god as pubescent, evokes that pubescence by giving the god a high and cracking voice. Suppose that instead of describing a character's tension over an uncertain outcome, the narrator evokes that tension by putting that character's actions into lines that dangle the action of a sentence over the brink of a pause before they reveal the result? And what if the narrator, instead of declaring the words of a particular character to be important, uses pitch and amplitude to mark them out as a steep-sided acoustical promontory among gently rolling hills?"

3. Zumthor, whose work I admire, sketches a somewhat more complex classification, establishing opposition between sacred and profane on one dimension and lyric versus narrative on another. In his scheme he aligns narrative with dramatic instead of against it, among other differences. See p. 76. I welcome such alternative suggestions; all together, they can add breadth to our capacity to appreciate Native American oral poetry and fit it properly into the grand scheme of humanity's triumphant artistic achievement.

BIBLIOGRAPHY

Abrams, George. 1967. "Moving the Fire: A Case of Iroquois Ritual Innovation," 23-24. In *Iroquois Culture, History and Prehistory*, ed. Elisabeth Tooker. Albany: New York State Museum and Science Service.

Alexander, Michael. 1966. *The Earliest English Poems*. Berkeley: University of California Press.

Altick, Richard D. 1957. *The English Common Reader: A Social History of the Mass Reading Public, 1800–1900*. Chicago: University of Chicago Press.

Astrov, Margot, ed. 1944; repr., 1962. *American Indian Prose and Poetry (The Winged Serpent)*. New York: John Day; repr., New York: Capricorn Books.

Bakhtin, M. M. 1981. *The Dialogic Imagination*. Austin: University of Texas Press.

Barnes, Nellie. 1922. *American Indian Verse, Characteristics of Style*. Lawrence: Bulletin of the University of Kansas, vol. 22, no. 18.

Basso, Keith. 1990. "Stalking With Stories," 98–137. In his *Western Apache Language and Culture*. Tucson: University of Arizona Press.

Bataille, Gretchen. 1983. "Transformation of Tradition: Autobiographical Works by American Indian Women." In *Studies in American Indian Literature*, ed. Paula Gunn Allen. New York: Modern Language Association of America.

Beck, Peggy, Anna Lee Walters, and Nia Francisco. 1990. *The Sacred: Ways of Knowledge, Sources of Life*. Flagstaff, Ariz.: Northland Publishing Co.

Bierhorst, John. 1974; repr., 1984. *Four Masterworks of American Indian Literature*. New York: Farrar, Straus and Giroux; repr., Tucson: University of Arizona Press.

———. 1985. *The Mythology of North America*. New York: William Morrow and Company.

Boas, Franz. 1940. *Race Language and Culture*. New York: Macmillan.

Bolton, W. F. 1982. *A Living Language: The History and Structure of English*. New York: Random House.

Booth, Mark W. 1981. *The Experience of Songs*. New Haven: Yale University Press.

Brady, Ivan, ed. 1991. *Anthropological Poetics*. Savage, Md.: Rowman and Littlefield.

Brandon, William. 1971. *The Magic World: American Indian Songs and Poems*. New York: William Morrow and Company.

Bright, William. 1984. *American Indian Linguistics and Literature*. Amsterdam: Mouton.

Brotherson, Gordon. 1992. *Book of the Fourth World: Reading the Native Americans through Their Literature*. New York: Cambridge University Press.

Bruner, Edward M., and Phyllis Gorfain. 1984. "Dialogic Narration and the Paradoxes of Masada." In *Text, Play and Story: The Construction and Reconstruction of Self and Society*, ed. Edward M. Bruner. Prospect Heights: Waveland Press.

Bunzel, Ruth. 1932. *Zuni Ritual Poetry*. Washington, D.C.: Bureau of American Ethnology Annual Report no. 47.

Canfield, William W., ed. 1971. *The Legends of the Iroquois Told by "The Cornplanter."* Empire State Historical Publication Series no. 93. Port Washington, N.Y.: Kennikat Press.

Carlyle, Thomas. 1915. "On History." *English and Other Critical Essays*. New York: Everyman's Library.

Chafe, Wallace L. 1961. *Seneca Thanksgiving Rituals*. Washington, D.C.: Bureau of American Ethnology Bulletin no. 183.

Chapman, Abraham, ed. 1975. *Literature of the American Indians: Views and Interpretations*. New York: New American Library.

Copway, George [Kah-Ge-Ga-Gah-Bowh]. 1850. *The Traditional History and Characteristic Sketches of the Objibway Nation*. London: Charles Gilpin.

Cronyn, George W. 1934; repr., 1963. *Path of the Rainbow: An Anthology of Songs and Chants from the Indians of North America*. New York: Liveright. Repr. as *American Indian Poetry: An Anthology of Songs and Chants*, New York: Ballatine.

Curtis, Natalie. 1907; repr., 1923. *The Indians' Book: Songs and Legends of the American Indian*. New York: Harper and Brothers.

Denig, Edwin T. 1930. *Indian Tribes of the Upper Missouri*. Washington, D.C.: Bureau of American Ethnology Annual Report no. 46.

Derrida, Jacques. 1976. *Of Grammatology*, trans. Gayatri Spivak. Baltimore: Johns Hopkins University Press.

Densmore, Frances. 1910. *Chippewa Music I*. Washington. D.C.: Bureau of American Ethnology Bulletin no. 45.

———. 1918. *Teton Sioux Music*. Washington, D.C.: Bureau of American Ethnology Bulletin no. 61.

Drabble, Margaret, ed. 1985. *The Oxford Companion to English Literature*. Oxford: Oxford University Press.

Eliot, T. S. 1952. *The Complete Poems and Plays: 1909-1950*. New York: Harcourt, Brace and Company.

Farella, John. 1993. *The Wind in a Jar*. Albuquerque: University of New Mexico Press.

Faris, James. 1990. *The Nightway: A History and a History of Documentation of a Navajo Ceremonial*. Albuquerque: University of New Mexico Press.

Farrer, Claire. 1992. *Living Life's Circle: Mescalero Apache Cosmovision*. Albuquerque: University of New Mexico Press.

Fenton, William N. 1978. "Northern Iroquoian Culture Patterns." In *Handbook of the Native American Indian*, vol. 15, ed. Bruce G. Trigger, Washington, D.C.: Smithsonian Institution.

Finnegan, Ruth. 1988. *Literacy and Orality: Studies in the Technology of Communication*. New York: Basil Blackwell.

Foster, Michael K. 1974. *From the Earth to Beyond the Sky: An Ethnographic Approach to Four Longhouse Iroquois Speech Events*. Ph.D. diss. University of Pennsylvania. Ann Arbor: Xerox University Microfilms 75-2728.

Franciscan Fathers. 1910. *An Ethnologic Dictionary of the Navajo Language*. Saint Michaels, Ariz.: Saint Michaels Press.

Frisbie, Charlotte J. 1980. *Southwestern Indian Ritual Drama*. Albuquerque: University of New Mexico Press.

Frye, Northrop. 1982. *The Great Code: The Bible and Literature*. New York: Harcourt Brace Jovanovich.

Gabel, John B., and Charles B. Wheeler. 1986. *The Bible as Literature: An Introduction*. New York: Oxford University Press.

Geertz, Clifford. 1957. "Ethos, World-view and the Analysis of Sacred Symbols." *Antioch Review* 17: 421–37.

Gelb, I. J. 1963. *A Study of Writing*, rev. ed. Chicago: University of Chicago Press.

Georges, Robert A. 1969. "Toward An Understanding of Storytelling Events." *Journal of American Folklore* 82: 314–28.

Ghezzi, Ridie Wilson. 1993. "Tradition and Innovation in Objibwe Storytelling," 36–37. In *New Voices in Native American Storytelling*, ed. Arnold Krupat. Washington, D.C.: Smithsonian Institution Press.

Gill, Sam. 1974. "A Theory of Navajo Prayer Acts: A Study in Ritual Symbolism." Ph.D. diss., University of Chicago.

———. 1981. *Sacred Words: A Study of Navajo Religion and Prayer*. Westport, Conn.: Greenwood Press.

Ginzburg, Carlo. 1980. *The Cheese and the Worms: The Cosmos of a Sixteenth Century Miller*. Baltimore: Johns Hopkins University Press.

Gleason, H. A., Jr. 1965. *Linguistics and English Grammar*. New York: Holt, Rinehart and Winston.

Goddard, Pliny Earle. 1933. *Navajo Texts*. Anthropological Papers, vol. 34. New York: American Museum of Natural History.

Goody, Jack, ed. 1968. *Literacy in Traditional Societies*. Cambridge: Cambridge University Press.

Greenblatt, Stephen. 1982. "Filthy Rites." *Daedelus* 3: 1–16.

Greenway, John. 1964. *Literature among the Primitives*. Hatboro, Pa.: Folklore Associates.

Gummere, Francis E. 1901. *The Beginnings of Poetry*. New York: Macmillan.

Haile, Berard. 1938. *Origin Legend of the Navajo Enemy Way*. Yale University Publications in Anthropology, No. 17. New Haven: Yale University Press.

———. 1981. *Women versus Men: A Conflict of Navajo Emergence*. Lincoln: University of Nebraska Press.

Hale, Horatio. 1883; repr., 1972. *The Iroquois Book of Rites*. Brinton's Library of

Aboriginal American Literature, No. 2. Philadelphia: D. G. Brinton. Facsimile ed. repr., Toronto: Coles Publishing Company.

Havelock, Eric. 1963. *Preface to Plato*. Cambridge: Harvard University Press.

———. 1976. *Origins of Western Literacy*. Toronto: Ontario Institute for Studies in Education.

Hewitt, J. N. B. 1903. *Iroquoian Cosmology*. Washington, D.C.: Bureau of American Ethnology Annual Report no. 21.

———. 1944. "The Requickening Address of the Iroquois Condolence Council." *Journal of the Washington Academy of Sciences* (March 15): 65–85.

Huntsman, Jeffrey F. 1979. "Traditional Native American Literature: The Translation Dilemma." *Shantih* 4, no. 2 (Summer-Fall): 5–9. Repr. in Swann (1983), 87–97.

Hymes, Dell. 1981. *"In Vain I Tried to Tell You"*: Essays in Native American Ethnopoetics. Philadelphia: University of Pennsylvania Press.

———. 1987. "Anthologies and Narratives," 41–84. In *Recovering the Word*: Essays on Native American Literature, ed. Brian Swann and Arnold Krupat. Berkeley: University of California Press.

Jahner, Elaine. 1983. "Stone Boy: Persistent Hero." In *Smoothing the Ground*: Essays on Native American Oral Literature, ed. Brian Swann. Berkeley: University of California Press.

Jason, Heda. 1972. "Jewish Near-Eastern Numbskull Tales: An Attempt at Interpretation. *Asian Folklore Studies* 31.

Johnny John, Richard. 1990. "Thank You: A Poem in Seventeen Parts," 4–11. In *Shaking the Pumpkin*, ed. Jerome Rothenberg. Albuquerque: University of New Mexico Press.

Jorgensen, Joseph G. 1992. Foreword to Anne M. Smith, *Ute Tales*. Salt Lake City: University of Utah Press.

Kaufmann, Michael. 1994. *Textual Bodies: Modernism, Postmodernism, and Print*. Lewisburg: Bucknell University Press.

King, Jeff, Maud Oakes, and Joseph Campbell. 1943. *Where the Two Came to Their Father*: A Navajo War Ceremonial. Bollingen Series I. New York: Pantheon Books.

Krupat, Arnold M. 1983. "The Indian Autobiography: Origins, Type, and Function," 261–82. In *Smoothing the Ground*: Essays on Native American Oral Literature, ed. Brian Swann. Berkeley: University of California Press.

———. 1992. "On the Translation of Native American Song and Story: A Theorized History," 3–28. In *On the Translation of Native American Literatures*, ed. Brian Swann. Berkeley: University of California Press.

———. 1993. *Ethnocriticism*: Ethnography, History, Literature. Berkeley: University of California Press.

Labov, William. 1972. "The Logic of Non-standard English" and "The Transformation of Experience in Narrative Syntax." In his *Language and the Inner City*. Philadelphia: University of Pennsylvania Press.

LaFlésche, Francis. 1925. *The Osage Tribe: The Right of Vigil*. Washington, D.C.: Bureau of American Ethnology 30th Annual Report.

———. 1939. *The War Ceremony of the Osage Indians*. Washington, D.C.: Bureau of American Ethnology 39th Annual Report.

Landau, Misia. 1991. *Narratives of Human Evolution*. New Haven: Yale University Press.

Laski, Vera. 1950; repr., 1972. *The Text of the Rain God Drama*, 214–35. In *Shaking the Pumpkin*, ed. Jerome Rothenberg. New York: Doubleday.

Lattimore, Richmond, trans. 1978. *Hesiod: The Works and Days, Theogeny, The Shield of Herakles*. Ann Arbor: University of Michigan Press.

Levenston, E. A. 1992. *The Stuff of Literature: Physical Aspects of Texts and Their Relations to Literary Meaning*. Albany: State University of New York Press.

Levy, Reuben, trans. 1967. *The Epic of the Kings: Shah-nama the National Epic of Persia by Ferdowsi*. Chicago: University of Chicago Press.

Lord, Albert M. 1960. *The Singer of Tales*. Cambridge: Harvard University Press.

Luckert, Karl. 1975. *The Navajo Hunter Tradition*. Tucson: University of Arizona Press.

———. 1976. *Olmec Religion: A Key to Middle America and Beyond*. Norman: University of Oklahoma Press.

———. 1979. *Coyoteway: A Navajo Holyway Healing Ceremonial*. Flagstaff: Museum of Northern Arizona Press.

Magoun, Francis P. 1953. "The Oral-Formulaic Character of Anglo-Saxon Narrative Poetry." *Speculum* 28: 446–67.

Malotki, Ekkehart. 1978. *Hopitutuwutsi: Hopi Tales*. Flagstaff: Museum of Northern Arizona Press.

Mallery, Garrick. 1972. *Picture Writing of the American Indians*. 2 vols. New York: Dover Publications. First published as the Tenth Annual Report of the Bureau of American Ethnology, 1888–89.

Martin, Henri-Jean. 1994. *The History and Power of Writing*. Chicago: University of Chicago Press.

Matthews, Washington. 1883–84. *The Mountain Chant: A Navajo Ceremony*. Washington, D.C.: Fifth Annual Report of the Bureau of American Ethnology.

———. 1885; repr., 1888, 1975. "Natural Naturalists." Philosophical Society of Washington, Bulletin 7. Repr. in Smithsonian Miscellaneous Collection, vol. 33, 1888; and in Robert Marshall Poor, *Washington Matthews: An Intellectual Biography* (Master's thesis, University of Nevada, Reno, 1975).

———. 1897; repr., 1993. *Navaho Legends*. Boston: American Folklore Society; repr., Salt Lake City: University of Utah Press.

———. 1902. *The Night Chant: A Navajo Ceremony*. Memoirs of the American Museum of Natural History, vol. 6. New York: Knickerbocker Press.

Michelson, Truman. 1937. *On the Fox Indians*. Washington, D.C.: Bureau of American Ethnography Fifth Annual Report.

Miller, Jay. 1991. *Oral Literature*. D'Arcy McNickle Center Occasional Papers Series no. 13. Chicago: Newberry Library.

Morgan, Lewis Henry. 1851; repr., 1962. *League of the Iroquois*. Rochester, N.Y.: Sage and Brother; repr., Secaucus, N.J.: Citadel Press.

Murie, James R. 1989. *Ceremonies of the Pawnee*. Ed. Douglas R. Parks. Lincoln: University of Nebraska Press.

Newcomb, Franc. 1967; repr., 1990. *Navajo Folk Tales*. Santa Fe: Museum of

Navajo Ceremonial Art; repr., Albuquerque: University of New Mexico Press.

Nichols, William. 1983. "Black Elk's Truth," 334–43. In *Smoothing the Ground*: *Essays on Native American Oral Literature*, ed. Brian Swann. Berkeley: University of California Press.

Ong, Walter. 1982. *Orality and Literacy*: *The Technologizing of the Word*. London: Methuen.

Ortiz, Alfonso. 1969. *The Tewa World*: *Space, Time, Being and Becoming in a Pueblo Society*. Chicago: University of Chicago Press.

Parker, Arthur C. 1916. *The Constitution of the Five Nations or the Iroquois Book of the Great Law*. Albany: New York State Museum Bulletin no. 184.

———. 1923; repr., 1989. *Seneca Myths and Folktales*. Buffalo: Buffalo Historical Society; repr., Lincoln: University of Nebraska Press.

Parks, Douglas R., ed. 1989. *Ceremonies of the Pawnee by James R. Murie*. Lincoln: University of Nebraska Press.

Powers, William K. 1992. "Translating the Untranslatable: The Place of Vocables in Lakota Song," 293–310. In *On the Translation of Native American Literature*, ed. Brian Swann. Washington D.C.: Smithsonian Institution Press.

Preminger, Alex, Frank Warnke, and O. B. Hardison, Jr., eds. 1990. *Princeton Encyclopedia of Poetry and Poetics*. Princeton, N.J.: Princeton University Press.

Radin, Paul. 1956. *The Trickster*. London: Routledge, Paul and Kegan.

Reichard, Gladys. 1944. *Prayer*: *The Compulsive Word*. New York: J. J. Augustin.

Rice, Julian. 1993. *Ellen Deloria's "The Buffalo People."* Albuquerque: University of New Mexico Press.

Rodgers, Glen, and Paul G. Zolbrod. 1989. "The Scientist as Storyteller, Storytelling as Science." *North Dakota Quarterly* 56.

Rosaldo, Renato. 1989. *Culture and Truth*: *The Remaking of Social Analysis*. Boston: Beacon Press.

Rothenberg, Jerome. 1972; rev. ed., 1990. *Shaking the Pumpkin*: *Traditional Poetry of the Indian North Americas*. Garden City, N.Y.: Doubleday; rev. ed., Albuquerque: University of New Mexico Press.

Sagan, Carl. 1980. *Cosmos*. New York: Random House.

Sandars, Thomas E., and Walter W. Peek. 1973. *Literature of the American Indian*. Beverly Hills: Glencoe Press.

Schoolcraft, Henry Rowe. 1853. *Western Scenes and Reminiscences*. Buffalo: Derby, Orton and Mulligan.

Shaul, David Leeson. 1992. "Hopi Song Poems in 'Context'," 228–241. In *On the Translation of Native American Literatures*, ed. Brian Swann. Washington, D.C.: Smithsonian Institution Press.

Sherzer, Joel. 1983. *Kuna Ways of Speaking*: *An Ethnographic Perspective*. Austin: University of Texas Press.

Sherzer, Joel, and Anthony C. Woodbury, eds. 1987. *Native American Discourse*: *Poetics and Rhetoric*. Cambridge: Cambridge University Press.

Shuman, Amy. 1986. *Storytelling Rights*: *The Uses of Oral and Written Texts by Urban Adolescents*. Cambridge: Cambridge University Press.

Smith, Anne. 1992. *Ute Tales*. Salt Lake City: University of Utah Press.

Spencer, Katherine. 1957. *Mythology and Values: An Analysis of Navaho Chantway Myths*. Philadelphia: American Folklore Society.

Spinden, Herbert. 1908. *The Nez Perce Indians*. Lancaster: American Anthropological Association Memoirs, vol. 2, pt. 3.

———. 1933. *Songs of the Tewa*. New York: Exposition of Indian Tribal Arts.

Stevenson, Maltilda Coxe. 1894. *The Zia*. Washington, D.C.: Eleventh Annual Report of the Bureau of Ethnology, 1889–1990.

Streit, Eloise. 1963. *Sepass Poems: The Songs of Y-Ail-Mihth*. New York: Vantage Press.

Swann, Brian. 1985. *Song of the Sky: Versions of Native American Songs and Poems*. Ashuelot, N.H.: Four Zoas Night House.

Swann, Brian, ed. 1983. *Smoothing the Ground: Essays on Native American Oral Literature*. Berkeley: University of California Press.

———. 1992. *On the Translation of Native American Literatures*. Washington, D.C.: Smithsonian Institution Press.

Swanton, Frank. 1909. *Tlingit Myths and Tales*. Washington, D.C.: Bureau of American Ethnology 39th Annual Report.

———. 1912. *Haida Songs*. Leiden: E. J. Brill.

Tedlock, Dennis. 1968. *The Ethnography of Tale-Telling at Zuni*. Ann Arbor, Mich.: University Microfilms.

———. 1971. "On the Translation of Style in Oral Narrative." *Journal of American Folklore* 84: 114–33. Reprinted in Swann (1983), pp. 57–77.

———. 1978. *Finding the Center*. Lincoln: University of Nebraska Press.

———. 1983. *The Spoken Word and the Work of Interpretation*. Philadelphia: University of Pennsylvania Press.

———. 1987. "Questions Concerning Dialogical Anthropology. *Journal of Anthropological Research* 43: 325—44.

——— 1991. "The Speaker of Tales Has More Than One String to Play On." In *Anthropological Poetics*, ed. Ivan Brady. Savage, Md.: Rowman and Littlefield.

Toelken, Barre, and Tacheeni Scott. 1981. "Poetic Retranslation and the 'Pretty Languages' of Yellowman." In *Traditional American Indian Literatures: Texts and Interpretations*, ed. Karl Kroeber. Lincoln: University of Nebraska Press.

Tooker, Elisabeth. 1978. "The Longhouse Religion," 454–65. In *Handbook of North American Indians*, vol. 15. Washington, D.C.: Smithsonian Institution.

Tooker, Elisabeth, ed. 1979. *Native North American Spirituality*. New York: Paulist Press.

Trimmer, Joseph F., and Maxine Hairston, eds. 1990. *The Riverside Reader*. Third Edition. Boston: Houghton Mifflin Company.

Twain, Mark (Samuel Clemens). 1985. *Adventures of Huckleberry Finn*. The Mark Twain Library. Berkeley: University of California Press.

Underhill, Ruth. 1936. *The Autobiography of a Papago Woman*. Menasha, Wisc.: American Anthropological Association Memoirs, vol. 46.

———. 1938. *Singing for Power: The Song Magic of the Papago Indians of Southern Arizona*. Berkeley: University of California Press.

Underhill, Ruth M., Donald M. Bahr, Baptisto Lopez, José Pancho and David Lopez. 1979. *Rainhouse and Ocean: Speeches for the Papago Year*. American Tribal Religions, vol. 4. Flagstaff: Museum of Northern Arizona Press.

Vico, Giambattista. 1968. *The New Science of Giambattista Vico*, trans. T. G. Bergin and Max Fisch.

Wallace, Anthony F. 1970. *The Death and Rebirth of the Seneca*. New York: Alfred A. Knopf.

Wallace, Paul A. W. 1946. *The White Roots of Peace*. Philadelphia: University of Pennsylvania Press; repr., Saranac Lake: Chauncy Press.

Welsh, Andrew. 1978. *The Roots of Lyric: Primitive Poetry and Modern Poetics*. Princeton: Princeton University Press.

Williams, Raymond. 1985. *Keywords: A Vocabulary of Culture and Society*. New York: Oxford University Press.

Wissler, Clark, and D. C. Duvall. 1908. *Mythology of the Blackfoot Indians*. New York: Anthropological Papers of the American Museum of Natural History.

Wordsworth, William. 1802; repr., 1967. "Observations Prefixed to 'Lyrical Ballads.'" In *The Great Critics: An Anthology of Literary Criticism*, ed. James Harry Smith and Edd Winfield Parks. New York: W. W. Norton and Company.

Wyman, Leland C. 1965. *The Red Antway of the Navajo*. Tucson: University of Arizona Press.

———. 1970. *Blessingway*. Tucson: University of Arizona Press.

Wyman, Leland C., and Clyde Kluckhohn. 1938. *Navaho Classification of Their Song Ceremonials*. Menasha, Wisc.: American Anthropological Association Memoir no. 50.

Zolbrod, Paul G. 1984. *Diné bahane': The Navajo Creation Story*. Albuquerque: University of New Mexico Press.

———. 1992a. "Cosmos and Poesis in the Seneca Thank-You Prayer." In *Earth and Sky: The Cosmos of the American Indian*, ed. Claire Farrer and Ray Williamson. Albuquerque: University of New Mexico Press.

———. 1992b. "Navajo Poetry in Print and in the Field: An Exercise in Text Retrieval." In *Essays on the Translation of Native American Literature*, ed. Brian Swann. Washington, D.C.: University Press of the Smithsonian Institution.

Zumthor, Paul. 1990. *Oral Poetry: An Introduction*. Minneapolis: University of Minnesota Press.